Old Wine

in

New Skins

The Aquinas Lecture, 2003

Old Wine
in
New Skins

The Role of Tradition in Communication,
Knowledge, and Group Identity

Jorge J. E. Gracia

MARQUETTE
UNIVERSITY

PRESS

BT90
.G68
2003
051210329

Under the auspices of the
Wisconsin-Alpha Chapter of Phi Sigma Tau

Library of Congress Cataloging-in-Publication Data

Gracia, Jorge J. E.
  Old wine in new skins : the role of tradition in com-
munication, knowledge, and group identity / by Jorge
J.E. Gracia.
    p. cm. — (The Aquinas lecture ; 2003)
"Under the auspices of the Wisconsin-Alpha Chapter of
Phi Sigma Tau."
Includes bibliographical references.
  ISBN 0-87462-170-4 (hardcover : alk. paper)
  1. Tradition (Theology) 2. Tradition (Philosophy) I.
Title. II. Series.
  BT90.G68 2003
  231'.042—dc21

                                        2002155115

© 2003 Marquette University Press
Printed in the United States of America

MARQUETTE UNIVERSITY PRESS
MILWAUKEE

The Association of Jesuit University Presses

Prefatory

The Wisconsin-Alpha Chapter of Phi Sigma Tau, the International Honor Society for Philosophy at Marquette University, each year invites a scholar to deliver a lecture in honor of St. Thomas Aquinas.

The 2003 Aquinas Lecture, *Old Wine in New Skins: The Role of Tradition in Communication, Knowledge, and Group Identity,* was delivered on Sunday, February 23, 2003, by Jorge J. E. Gracia, the Samuel P. Capen Chair and SUNY Distinguished Professor at the University of Buffalo.

Jorge Gracia earned a B.A. from Wheaton College, an M.A. from the University of Chicago, an M.S.L. from the Pontifical Institute of Mediaeval Studies, and a Ph.D. from the University of Toronto. Besides his distinguished career at the State University of New York at Buffalo, Professor Gracia has been visiting professor at Universidad de Puerto Rico in 1972-1973, at Instituto de Investigaciones Filosóficas, Universidad Nacional Autónoma de México in June of 1984, at Universidad de Michoacán in 1996, at Franciscan University in 1997, at Fordham University in 1997, and at Internationale Akademie für Philosophie, Liechtenstein, in 1998.

Professor Gracia has been president of the Society for Medieval and Renaissance Philosophy from 1991 to1993, of the Society for Iberian and Latin American Thought from 1986 to 1988, of the Federación International de Estudios sobre América Latina y el

Caribe from 1987 to 1989, of the American Catholic Philosophical Association from 1997 to 1998, and of the Metaphysical Society of America from 2000 to 2001.

Professor Gracia's most recent books include *How Can We Know What God Means? The Interpretation of Revelation* (2001), *Hispanic/Latino Identity: A Philosophical Perspective* (2000), *Metaphysics and Its Task: The Search for the Categorial Foundation of Knowledge* (1999), *Filosofía hispánica: Concepto, origen y foco historiográfico* (1998), *Texts: Ontological Status, Identity, Author, Audience* (1996), *A Theory of Textuality: The Logic and Epistemology* (1995), and *Philosophy and Its History: Issues in Philosophical Historiography* (1992). He has also translated two volumes of the *Metaphysical Disputations* of Francisco Suárez and edited, alone or with others, eighteen books, as well as special journal issues on the transcendentals in medieval philosophy, on Francisco Suárez, and on Latin American philosophy today.

Professor Gracia has one hundred and ninety-two articles in print, mainly in medieval and in Latin-American philosophy, metaphyscis, and hermeneutics. His list of papers presented numbers close to two hundred. His service to the profession of philosophy during his distinguished career is exemplary.

To Professor Gracia's impressive list of publications, Phi Sigma Tau is pleased to add: *Old Wine in New Skins: The Role of Tradition in Knowledge, Communication, and Group Identity.*

For Clarisa the Younger and James the Good

Because of our traditions we've
kept our balance for many years ….
Because of our traditions, everyone
here knows who he is and what God
expects him to do.

Tevye, *Fiddler on the Roof*

Contents

Preface

The importance of tradition can hardly be overstated. Tradition seems to be at the core of human actions, culture, beliefs, and values; it is both the lifeline and the foundation of society; and it functions as a flexible glue that binds communities. There is practically no dimension of human activity that is not in some way related to, and influenced by, tradition. Tradition permeates our lives and helps explain much that otherwise would be mystifying. What is religion without tradition, for example?[1] Can nations endure without traditions? And where would institutions, universities, and associations be without traditions? Indeed, one is justified in asking whether they can exist at all outside traditions. Furthermore, is it possible to understand the many moral precepts that govern our lives, most rules of etiquette by which we regulate social interactions, and a good number of the desires we feel without reference to tradition? Consider the Chinese principle that we should honor our ancestors; the English custom of using formulas such as 'Good morning,' 'Thank you,' and 'You are welcome'; and the desire of Cubans to eat roast pork on Christmas Eve. Can we make sense of any of these without reference to tradition?

But we need not restrict ourselves to these categories, for many other dimensions of our ordinary behavior make no sense without reference to tradition. Many other things we do can be explained through tradition. For example, I may not particularly like, nor is it my duty, to eat turkey on Thanksgiving, but I do it, at least in part, because this is a tradition I accept. There is no moral compulsion to celebrate birthdays, but we do it again in part out of respect for a well-established tradition. And we can go even further, for human experience itself seems to be molded and informed by tradition.[2] The way we grasp the significance of certain situations and actions is often affected by tradition. For example, in the re-enactment of the Last Supper, Baptists consider the bread a symbol of Christian unity, but Roman Catholics believe it is the body of Christ, and this is a matter of tradition.

These are just some of the many ways in which tradition affects us, but there is another aspect of tradition that we should not forget: In a world in which the process of globalization is increasingly evident, where the forces that affect and sometimes even shape our lives are mostly out of our control, and where our identity as individuals often gets lost in the commotion that characterizes contemporary human society, tradition provides a measure of meaning and stability, or perhaps even the only meaning and stability that some of us may have.[3] Tradition serves to ground and preserve our identity by locating us within smaller communities with which we can identify, in which our voices can be heard, and whose perspectives we accept and share.

Yet, although tradition permeates our lives, dictating much of what we do and explaining social phenomena that would otherwise defy understanding, it is neither a well-studied topic nor uncontroversial. References to tradition and claims about it abound, but it is shocking to find that only one systematic and general book has been written about it, and that it is of relatively recent origin.[4] Of course, there are many books and articles on various specific aspects of tradition, on particular traditions, or on different kinds of traditions. In political and religious contexts, for example, there have been long-standing controversies about the attitude we should adopt toward tradition, the way we should understand it, and its role in human affairs. Discussions of these topics are common among Roman Catholic and Protestant theologians, for example. But tradition, *qua* tradition, has not often been the subject of philosophical discussion and never the object of an extended systematic inquiry, even though some of the titles of many specific studies misleadingly suggest otherwise.[5] This means, of course, that confusions about it abound and it is difficult even to sort out the proper issues that should be raised in connection with it. It is particularly surprising that, although tradition is a social phenomenon, very few social scientists have ventured to study it in depth.[6]

There is more to this state of affairs than neglect, for tradition is a very controversial topic. Indeed, it might be precisely its controversial nature that has made so many shy away from its investigation. Even the mere use of the word 'tradition' evokes strong and contradictory reactions. In some cases, to speak of tradition makes people think positively about much that they value, but in other cases, it elicits negative responses, making them feel trapped in what they consider to be meaningless and counter-productive rigmaroles. For some, tradition is the basis of what is most important and meaningful in human lives; tradition helps preserve identity and justifies ways of living that are dear to them.[7] For others, however, tradition is a synonym of 'dogma' and regarded as something dead, that does not any longer provide significance to their existence but rather traps them in oppressive confines.[8] Indeed, for some tradition smacks of superstition, irrationality, and an anti-scientific spirit, an attitude which no doubt can be traced to the Enlightenment and its hostility to anything that is not directly related to reason.[9] Finally, in some recent discussions, tradition has been associated with what is socially elitist and politically reactionary, that is, with ways used by dominant groups to preserve privilege and exclude the disadvantaged and marginalized from sharing in the goods of particular societies. As such, it is also often presented as an obstacle to individual freedom and even to the proper development of personal maturity and individuality.[10]

    Context has much to do with what people think and feel when they hear or use the word 'tradition.'

In certain religious circles, such as Roman Catholic, Jewish, and Muslim, tradition is seen as essential to religious faith, but for some Evangelical Christians, tradition can be an obstacle to the proper understanding of Christ's message as revealed in the Christian Scriptures.[11] Because these contexts vary considerably and their examination is not required for my purposes, I do not explore them here. For my immediate aims, we need only look at tradition from a general philosophical perspective. But even in philosophy, reactions to tradition frequently differ. There is a long list of political philosophers, such as Jean-Jacques Rousseau, who regard tradition as nothing more than entrenched privilege and as standing in the way of social development and progress. Others, however, such as Edmund Burke, find in tradition the very foundation of community life, without which society would fall apart.

In philosophy, the notion of tradition has been used to deal with various puzzling problems. Three of these are particularly significant and will be taken up here. One has to do with communication;[12] another with the transmission of knowledge;[13] and the third with the identity of social groups.[14] In order for tradition to do the work it is asked to do in these contexts, it must make sense of continuity within change. Yet, this seems to be impossible if tradition is conceived in the way in which it is most often understood, namely, as a set of beliefs or doctrines. As a way to avoid this difficulty, and contrary to this widespread opinion, I propose rather that tradition needs to be understood, strictly speaking, as a kind of action or actions.

I proceed, first, by raising the three problems mentioned. Then, I look into the kind of identity that applies to tradition, for in all three cases, a major obstacle to the effective use of tradition appears to come from the difficulty of accounting for its identity through time. This in turn leads to a discussion of the factors that are part of the structure of tradition. The view that tradition consists of beliefs is criticized next and, in its place, I propose a view of it as action, distinguishing it further from habits, dispositions, and customs. Then I show how this conception helps to solve the problems of communication, the transmission of knowledge, and social group identity raised at the beginning. A short conclusion ends the discussion.

Before I begin, however, let me thank Bruce Reichenbach and George Allan, as well as my former students, Robert Delfino, Michael Gorman, William Irwin, John Kronen, Elizabeth Millán-Zaibert, Peter Redpath, and Jonathan Sanford, for the time and effort they devoted to reading and criticizing drafts of this lecture. I am greatly indebted to them for their many valuable suggestions and criticisms. Their perceptive and frank challenges prevented me from falling into a multitude of errors. I must also thank my research assistant, Brock Dereck, who read the manuscript with care, raised pertinent questions, and helped locate some sources.

1

Some Problems with Communication, Knowledge, and Group Identity

Tradition has been used to solve many important philosophical problems, including the mentioned three that have to do with communication, knowledge, and group identity. All three are fundamental and frequently thought to defy solution. Communication is the most basic, for the transmission of knowledge is closely connected with it, and the problem posed by group identity is parochial to certain specific issues related to social reality. I begin with communication.

A. Communication

Communication presents us with one of the most puzzling problems we encounter. It may be formulated in a general question: How is it possible? Or we could put it more concretely by asking: How do I know what you think, and how do you know what I think? Obviously, we use language to communicate with each other. I know that you think having a high-cholesterol diet is bad because you have told me so. The problem, of course, is to explain how I know this from the sounds you utter when you tell me, for the sounds themselves do not appear to have any obvious or natural connection to the thoughts they are used to convey. How can I know, then, that they convey those thoughts and not others? And the same applies to you and your knowledge of what I think.

One way in which this puzzle has been formulated is known as the Hermeneutic Circle.[15] This conundrum suggests that we are trapped in, and cannot escape, language and thus that we can never get at the thoughts which the use of language is supposed to convey. The meaning of language can be conveyed only through language. To explain what I mean by a linguistic term, I must use other linguistic terms. And to explain what I mean by these other linguistic terms, I must in turn use some other terms, and so on, *ad infinitum*, or back to the original *explanandum*. To convey what I mean by 'cat,' I need to use some other expression, such as 'feline mammal that meows.' But this itself, as a piece of language, requires an explanation, which again must be linguistic, and so on. In short, we are linguistically trapped and can never get to meanings or to thoughts.

This difficulty was identified by Augustine in *De Magistro*, where he put it with his characteristic simplicity and clarity as follows: "If I am given a sign and I do not know the thing of which it is the sign, it can teach me nothing. If I know the thing, what do I learn from the sign?"[16] In short, signs by themselves do not have the power to communicate, for either I know what they mean, and then their use tells me nothing that I did not already know, or I do not know what they mean, and then they do not communicate anything at all to me. Language by itself is helpless; it has no power to do what we need it to do. So how do we communicate?

One response to the Hermeneutic Circle is to argue that there are other, non-linguistic ways that explain communication. The most often pointed to of these are intuition and ostension. I know what you mean when you tell me something because either the meaning is intuitively revealed to me in a kind of epiphany or it is made plain by your pointing it to me. Neither of these, however, can defeat the Circle. An intuition is something too private to be of any use. It is for me alone and so it cannot explain how communication happens between two or more persons. Besides, the claim that intuition serves to communicate goes contrary to our common experience, for we do not always agree on meanings, and this implies that only some of us are privileged to intuit whatever the proper or real ones are, but this entails that intuition cannot serve to establish what each of us means when we speak. Clearly, this explanation does not take us beyond the realm of privacy, and hence it cannot help us solve the hermeneutic conundrum.

Ostension is not more helpful, for it suffers from many well-known problems, three of which are particularly serious: imprecision, indeterminacy, and circularity. When I want to communicate the meaning of 'cat' ostensibly to someone who does not know what the term means, I proceed by pointing to a cat. But this is not very helpful, for the person in question cannot tell whether I am pointing to the whole cat, a part of the cat, a property of the cat, or something in the neighborhood of the cat, to mention just a few of the most obvious possibilities involved. Clearly, pointing is a very imprecise procedure. But let us assume that none of this constitutes an insurmountable problem and that I have succeeded in getting the person for the benefit of whom I am pointing to see that I am pointing to the cat as a whole. Nonetheless, this is not enough, for the person still cannot tell how it is in particular that I want her to think about the cat. Do I have in mind a substance, a series of states, a bundle of properties, an event, or what? The reason this is a problem is that if one cannot determine how one is thinking of X, it might not be clear that one is actually thinking about it. This indicates that ostension is not sufficiently determinate. Finally, we should note that pointing itself is a sign, and this entails that it has a meaning on which we must agree for it to be effective in communication. But if this is true, then clearly, what was said about linguistic terms applies to it, and in using it I have only succeeded, in the best of cases, in substituting one term, 'cat,' for another, the act of pointing. So, the Hermeneutic Circle kicks in, for now I must communicate the meaning of the act of pointing, and how is this to be accomplished?

Elsewhere, I have suggested that an initial effective step in breaking the Circle is through the use of the notion of expected behavior.[17] I expect certain behavior from those with whom I am trying to communicate, and when this behavior takes place,

I know, with various degrees of certainty, that someone has understood what I have said, or that I have
understood what someone else has said to me. Consider the following exchange in a Mexican restaurant
in Milwaukee:

> I say: "Do you have *tamales*?"
> The waiter responds: "Yes."
> I: "What kind do you have?"
> Waiter: "*Chiapanecos, de bola*, and with *chipi-
> lín*."
> I: "Are the *chiapanecos* any good?"
> Waiter: "Yes, but I especially recommend the
> ones with *chipilín*. They are delicious."
> I: "I haven't had those. What kind of filling to
> they have?"
> Waiter: "Chicken or cheese."
> I: OK. Bring me some with cheese."
> Waiter: Yes, sir. Would you like something to
> drink with the *tamales*?"
> I: "Yes, bring me a Corona. Thanks."

At every point of this conversation, there are certain
behavioral expectations on the part of both the waiter
and me, and the satisfaction of these expectations are
essential to understanding on the part of the speakers
and the continuation of the dialogue. When I ask the
first question, there are three answers I expect: "Yes,"
"No," or "I don't know." All three suggest to me that
the waiter understands me. If instead of these, the
waiter says something like, "The weather is fine,"

"You are stupid," or "Life is a dream," for example, I would surmise he does not understand me, he did not hear me, he understands me but does not want to answer my question, or some such reason. And something similar can be said about the subsequent exchanges in the dialogue. When I ask about the kinds of *tamales* available, I am given a list of names some of which I recognize, and some of which I do not. And even when I do not know exactly what an answer means—say, about the kind of filling—the response is within parameters that make sense to me. If the waiter says the filling consists in diamonds, dirt, or water, I would immediately suspect a breakdown in communication or some other anomaly. So, let us assume that behavioral expectations help to explain how communication happens. Even then, it should be obvious that it is not enough to explain it, for a key question remains unanswered: Where do the expectations come from?

Many answers may be given to this question. For example, one may say that expectations are part of human nature. But this does not seem to work in the case we are considering insofar as the exchange described has to do with culture, not nature. That a restaurant has or does not have *tamales*, and a waiter answers my questions about *tamales* in a certain way, depends on cultural conventions.

One could also answer that expectations are grounded on intuitions. Again, however, this seems unsatisfactory in that such intuitions would themselves require explanation unless they were common to all humans. But it is clear that they are not. Indeed, the expectations that govern my exchange with the waiter cannot be explained in terms of anything that is common to all humans, for they are peculiar to the culture in which the exchange takes place and the elements that make up culture are not generally common to all persons, even if some may be. This should be rather obvious when we consider that the expectations of the participants in the dialogue are linguistic and concern a particular language, namely, English. This dialogue could not have taken place in Mexico among non-English-speaking Mexicans. There I would not have begun by asking in English, "Do you have *tamales*?" Rather, I would have begun by saying: "*¿Tiene tamales*?" The expectations, then, belong to the realm of culture and as such they are governed by customs that belong to a particular culture.

Here is where tradition comes in. Broadly speaking, we could say that it is traditional that, when one asks a waiter whether he has *tamales*, he will understand this to be a question as to whether the restaurant for which he works has *tamales* to be served and he will also understand that there are only certain answers that he is supposed to use in his response if he wishes or intends for me to understand him. And the same goes for the answers he gives, as well as for the questions I pose. Traditions teach us to expect certain behavior when there is common understanding and communication is achieved. From all this, it should be clear that traditions are closely related to customs, but I shall leave the task of pointing out their differences for chapter 5. It should also be obvious that what I have said so far is not enough to defeat the objection based on the Hermeneutic Circle; for that much more is needed, as will become clear later.

B. Knowledge

The problem with knowledge that concerns us in this context has to do with its transmission and is similar to the difficulty posed by communication. Hence, I do not need to give as much attention to its formulation as I gave to the problem of communication.

The transmission of knowledge is essential to civilization, for humans cannot build on a past that has not been preserved and passed on. Most knowledge is cumulative and depends on prior achievements. But how is this cumulative record transmitted? The obvious answer is that it is through texts, for although societies may transmit knowledge in many different ways, all of them involve the use of texts—by a text I mean a group of entities, used as signs, which are selected, arranged, and intended by an author in a certain context to convey some specific meaning to an audience.[18] I know the discoveries of the past through the texts that record them, whether this record is written or is part of a memory passed on orally. But how can I access those discoveries through texts, and how can I be certain that I have actually accessed them? How do I know that you and I understand what Calderón de la Barca meant when he wrote the famous words, "Life is a dream," when the framers of the American Declaration of Independence wrote, "All men are created equal," or when Einstein proposed the formula "$E = mc^2$"? How do I know that 'dream,' 'equal,' and 'E' mean what I understand by them?

Some think that we cannot know it; we can never be certain that what someone understands by a word is also understood by someone else. The reason is that we can only observe the behavior of those who use words and not what they think. In Quine's notorious example, when some tribal person whose language I do not know points to a rabbit going by and tells me "Gavagai," how do I know that my interlocutor means "rabbit"? [19] This problem is similar to the one we saw earlier in the context of communication. 'Gavagai' conveys no information to me about what my interlocutor means, because the only thing to which I have access, Quine would argue, is the behavior of the person who says "Gavagai," that is, his saying it. But this tells me nothing about what he means. Recall Augustine! Moreover, this difficulty becomes even more serious when we are dealing with a textual record from the past.

Obviously, in the transmission of knowledge, we have a problem similar to that posed by the Hermeneutic Circle for communication, so, presumably, we can also use the notions of expected behavior and tradition to solve it. Whether they are effective or not remains to be determined, however.

C. Group Identity

Finally, we have the problem of accounting for the development and preservation of the identity of social groups, such as ethnic groups and nations. What is it that unites ethnic groups, such as Hispanics? The members of this group are separated in location, time, race, and so on. Some Hispanics lived one-hundred years ago, whereas others are currently alive some reside in Cuba and some reside in Mexico; and some are Black and some are White. Indeed, there seems to be no property that ties the members of ethnic groups.[20] Although there may be some properties at certain times and places that appear to unite them, these do not extend beyond particular spatio-temporal coordinates. Even the most common cultural traits, such as language, and political organization, territory, self-awareness, and race, fail to extend to all members of these groups throughout their history. So, where can we find the unity, the elements that bind ethnic groups and account for their identity, when there is no common property to all the persons whom, throughout history, we identify as members of these groups?

The same applies, *mutatis mutandis*, to nations, such as Americans. Is there any property that characterizes all Americans *qua* Americans throughout their history, distinguishing them from non-Americans? Some might cite the adherence to the Constitution, but this is a text and is subject to the same hermeneutical problems we saw earlier—as a text we do not know that those who understand it understand the same thing by it. Shall we say, then, that what Americans share is a political organization? Not quite, for the political system of the United States seems to have evolved throughout the history of the country, and even though it may not have changed fundamentally, the interpretations of what it means have certainly changed—note for example how differently suffrage has been understood at different times. Perhaps we can cite citizenship. But here again it is not clear that this qualifies as a common property, for both the understanding of citizenship and the means to acquire it have evolved. So what is common to all Americans as such? Nothing very obvious, it seems, for Americans come in all colors, levels of intelligence, physical characteristics, beliefs, and so on, which means that the burden of proof is on those who think there is such a common property.

One way to account for the identity of groups is through tradition, assuming that tradition itself is not understood as a property, something that makes sense, for tradition is not anything like, say, color or height. Accordingly, although members of social groups may differ in significant ways, one could argue that there is a core of tradition that helps to tie them together into groups. Tradition, then, could play a key role in the understanding of group identity, just as we saw it could in communication and the transmission of knowledge. The exact nature of this role, however, requires further determination, something I shall attempt to provide later.

D. The Underlying Difficulty

In all three problems cited, tradition is proposed as a way to surmount gaps: Traditions are supposed to serve as bridges between language and thoughts, past knowledge and present awareness of it, and the differences that separate individual members within social groups. But how is it that traditions can do this? What are the conditions that traditions must satisfy in order for them to carry out this function?

If tradition is to help account effectively for how communication, the transference of knowledge, and group identity occur, it must satisfy at least one fundamental condition, namely, it must preserve its own identity through time. Why? Because in all three problematic cases cited, the function of tradition would appear to be to tie together disparate elements across time: what X thinks he means when he composes or uses text T at t_1 and what Y thinks T means when she reads it at t_2; awareness of a piece of knowledge P by X at t_1 and awareness of P by Y at t_2; and individual persons X, Y, and Z at t_1 and at t_2. In order for tradition to tie these and to function as a bridge between them, tradition itself would appear to need to maintain its own identity at the pertinent times.

Yet, this seems impossible, because the tension between sameness and difference, continuity and discontinuity, the old and the new, and coercion and freedom in tradition, seems to pose unresolvable antinomies.[21] Indeed, in certain fields, like literature and the arts, it is of the essence of tradition to go beyond what has been handed down. As T. S. Eliot puts it, "What happens [in the creative act of the artist] is a continual surrender of himself as he is at the moment to something which is more valuable. The progress of an artist is a continual self-sacrifice, a continual extinction of personality," for "he can neither take the past as a lump. . . nor can he form himself wholly on one or two private admirations."[22] And, even outside the arts, tradition appears to require openness: Tradition is not merely an inheritance from the past, but requires adoption and this involves much more than mere inheritance.[23] A tradition is not, as Eliot put it, merely a lump of something that is given to us; it has to be "incorporated," as some of those who speak of it often say, by which I take them to mean that traditions are made part of ourselves, and this entails change.[24] But, then, how can they have the identity they require to solve the problems to which I have referred?

2
The Identity of Tradition

An understanding of how tradition can be used in the solution to the problems of communication, the transmission of knowledge, and group identity necessitates that we determine the conditions of its own identity. But this in turn requires that we have at least a working understanding of identity and how it can apply to tradition.[25]

A. Identity

Identity, also referred to as sameness, is closely related to similarity. Indeed, it is not unusual to find authors who use 'identical' (or its rough synonym, 'same') and 'similar' interchangeably. This is so because in ordinary language we in fact use these terms interchangeably on some occasions. For example, we sometimes say that two blue-colored objects have identical color, even though the shades of blue in question might be different. In this sense, there is no difference between identity and similarity. But it is likewise true that we often entertain and use notions of identity and similarity which are different from each other. Indeed, in the very example just used, we also say that the two blue-colored objects are similar in color precisely because the particular shades of blue they have are different.

Among the important distinctions that can be made between the notions of identity and similarity, perhaps a key one is that similarity occurs always in the context of difference. Two things are similar only if they are also different in some respect, although the difference in question must refer to aspects other than those on which the similarity is based. Thus one may speak of two persons as being similar provided that they differ in some way. If they do not differ in any way, then they are regarded as identical, that is, as the same person. The conditions of similarity of two things, say X and Y, may be expressed in the following way:

> X is similar to Y, if and only if X and Y: (1) have at least one feature that is identical in both and (2) also have at least one feature that is not identical in both.

For the sake of convenience, features are understood very broadly in this formulation. They may include anything that may be said of a thing and thus not only qualities, but also relations, position, temporal location, states, actions, and so on.

Now, in contrast with similarity, identity does not require—indeed it precludes—difference. This does not mean that two things could not be regarded as identical, or as the same, with respect to some feature or other and different with respect to something else. A grand-daughter, for example, may be identical to her grandfather in temperament although she is different from him in gender. The point is, however, that for the grand-daughter and the grandfather to be the same with respect to temperament, their temperament must not be different in any way. If there were some difference, so that one were, say, volatile and the other not, one would more properly speak instead of a "similarity of temperament." We might express this understanding of the identity of two things, say X and Y, and the identity of their features in the following two propositions:

> X is the same as, or identical with, Y, if and only if there is nothing that pertains to X that does not pertain to Y, and vice versa.[26]

> X is the same as, or identical to, Y, with respect to a particular feature F, if and only if there is nothing that pertains to F in X that does not pertain to F in Y, and vice versa.

The first formula expresses *absolute identity,* because it applies to the whole entity in question; the second expresses *relative identity*, because it applies only to some feature(s) or aspect(s) of an entity.[27] In addition to these, however, one often finds authors who speak of identity in the way I have conceived similarity. And there are some that are willing to speak of identity when not even the conditions of similarity are met. To keep the latter two from being confused with the former two, I shall refer to the first of them as the *identity of similarity*, and to the second as *pseudo-identity*.

Part of the reason for the frequent blurring of the distinction between identity and similarity in English discourse is that a single term 'difference' is often used as the opposite of both, even though there exists another term that more properly expresses the opposite of similarity: 'dissimilarity.' Similar/different and identical/different are generally regarded as pairs of opposites in English. This usage does not necessarily extend to other languages, however. In the Middle Ages, for example, some effort was made to keep the notions of similarity and identity separate, and this was supported by the use of two different opposite terms for each. 'Difference' (*differentia*) was used, at least in most technical philosophical discourse, as the opposite of 'similarity' (*similaritas*), whereas 'diversity' (*diversitas*) was used as the opposite of 'identity' (*identitas*).[28]

The notion of identity presupposes that of non-identity.[29] The identity of X with Y implies its non-identity with non-Y, and the non-identity of X with Y implies its identity with itself. These notions are interdependent in the same way that the notions of cat and non-cat are; cat is significant as long as non-cat is, and vice versa.

Not all identity about which we speak is of the same sort, however. There are at least four fundamental but distinct kinds of identity: *achronic, synchronic, diachronic,* and *panchronic*.[30] *Achronic identity* is identity irrespective of time (as in "X is identical with Y"), whereas synchronic, diachronic, and panchronic identity involve time. *Synchronic identity* applies at a particular time (as in "X is identical with Y at t_1"); diachronic identity applies at two (or more, but not all) times (as in "X is identical with Y at t_1 and t_2"), and *panchronic identity* applies at all times (as in "X is identical with Y at every t").

These four kinds of identity generate four different problems for those who wish to account for each kind. Because my concern here is with the question of the identity of tradition over time, I deal exclusively with the problems raised by diachronic identity. In this kind of identity, what is at stake is the determination of the necessary and sufficient conditions that make a thing the same at two (or more, but not all) times. What is it that makes President Bush the same on the day of his inauguration and now? Indeed, it is usual for philosophers to speak of the problem of accounting for diachronic identity as the problem of accounting for "personal identity through time" or as the problem of "temporal continuity."[31] Diachronic identity applies only to those entities to which temporal passage applies. It makes no sense to talk about the diachronic identity of atemporal entities.

B. The Identity of Tradition

Now that we have working notions of identity and diachronic identity, we can apply them to tradition. And let me begin with the first. What we seek in this case is a set of conditions: necessary condi-

tions without which a tradition is not what it is and
sufficient conditions that distinguish one tradition
from all others. From what was said earlier, it follows
furthermore that, if there is identity of a tradition,
in a plural world such as ours this very fact implies
two others: the identity of something else and the
non-identity of the tradition with it. For, what constitutes the identity of one tradition is also presumably what sets it apart from other things, including
other traditions.[32] Identity, then, is bound up with
difference, a claim that should be understood both
metaphysically and epistemically: Metaphysically, it
means that identity and non-identity (or difference)
are interdependent; epistemically, it means that the
understanding of identity is bound up with the
understanding of non-identity.

The reference to metaphysical and epistemological
claims brings up another propaedeutic matter that
should be mentioned: The distinction between the
problem involved in accounting for identity and the
problem involved in accounting for the discernibility
of identity. The problem of identity is metaphysical,
having to do with what a thing is, apart from the
way we may think of it. Its solution, if there is one,
consists in the determination of the necessary and
sufficient conditions of the identity of the thing in
question. The problem of the discernibility of identity, on the other hand, is epistemological insofar as
it involves the determination of the necessary and
sufficient conditions of our knowledge of identity.

The metaphysical question that concerns us, then, involves an inquiry into the necessary and sufficient conditions of the *identity* of traditions, whereas the epistemological question involves an inquiry into the necessary and sufficient conditions for the *identification* of traditions, that is, the conditions that enable a knower to identify them. One point that needs to be kept in mind is that the logical distinction between these issues does not mean that the metaphysical conditions of identity may not play a role in the epistemic process of identification, or that the epistemic conditions of identification may not affect identity. Indeed, both do so, and often. What something is constitutes the foundation of what we know about it; and that we know it, and how, may affect what it is. This is most clear in the case of our own selves, because what we are determines what we can know about ourselves, and what we know about ourselves influences what we are.

To keep these two questions separate and avoid unnecessary complications when answering them, I prefer to refer to the second issue as *the problem of identification*, and to the first as *the problem of identity*.[33] Moreover, when the identification in question involves different times, that is, diachronic identity, I refer to the search for its necessary and sufficient conditions as *the problem of reidentification*.

So much for identity in general. Now let us turn to the question that is particularly pertinent for us here: Do traditions preserve their identity through time? Some empirical evidence seems to suggest that they do not. Although some authors claim they do, an unbiased investigation often reveals that traditions evolve and change. Indeed, the changes over time can be so drastic that over long periods some traditions become something quite different from, and even incompatible with, what they originally were. For example, the original meaning of words is often completely lost, and it does not take long for this to happen. Consider the common way of referring to what we now generally call fresh water, that is non-sea water. In the nineteenth century the favored term was 'sweet water,' but that is now unusual, at least in the United States.

But if it is true that traditions evolve and change in such radical ways, how can they function as bridges that solve the three problems to which reference was made earlier? Can traditions change as much as this and still provide a diachronic tie? How can they help us understand the way we communicate through texts, become aware of past discoveries, and account for the identity of social groups?

Some philosophers believe that there is no problem here insofar as these three phenomena are in fact mere illusions. According to them, we never know what others think when they speak to us; we never know what was actually discovered in the past; and the identity of social groups is a mere fancy. All three positions are common and have been defended by epistemologists, hermeneuticists, and social philosophers. The first has always been the province of the skeptics. Indeed, this is the position that Gorgias took in ancient Greece: Knowledge of what others think is not possible because communication is impossible.[34] The second is common among historicists, for if every moment of history is unique and irreproducible, then two instances of the same thought are impossible.[35] And the third has become quite fashionable today among those who regard social realities as fictions that are the result of social factors.[36]

But surely these are extreme views that go contrary to some of our most basic intuitions and much that we take for granted in our ordinary lives. If nothing else, they appear to be no more than poses in the face of the seeming inexplicability of these phenomena. So, if a way can be found to explain and understand the phenomena in question, there is no reason to take the skeptical route.

The key question for us, then, is the following: Can traditions help us explain communication, the transmission of knowledge, and social identity? Obviously, the answer requires an understanding of tradition that helps us do so, which is in fact our main task. I begin with an analysis of the various factors that play roles in tradition, what I call its "inner springs."

3
The Inner Springs of Tradition

Considering the importance of tradition in human affairs, one would have expected to find a viable understanding of it in the pertinent literature, but there is nothing of the kind. I find three difficulties with the treatments of tradition I have examined. Some develop views that are unacceptable either because they are clearly inadequate to account for our experience of tradition or because they are too vague to be of any use. Others do not settle on one way of understanding tradition, but go on describing it in so many different ways that it is impossible to determine exactly what the view proposed is. And still others ignore the many factors that seem to be intrinsically related to, and play roles in, tradition, thus presenting us with a distorted portrayal of it. So, let me begin with the analysis of these factors and then examine how they generate various views of tradition.

A. Factors that Play a Role in Tradition

It might be useful to begin by saying something about the origins of the word 'tradition.' Etymologically, the English term derives from the Latin *traditio*, which is a noun derived in turn from the verb *tradere* which means to transmit, transfer, or deliver. A *traditio* for the Romans consisted in the action of handing over something, of transferring something to someone else. The term was used in a legal context, for example, when the transfer of a house to new owners was accompanied by the action of handing over the keys to them (*traditio clavium*). But the Latin term was not used exclusively for the transference of objects. The verb *tradere* was also frequently used to mean "teaching," so that transmitting knowledge to someone was also called a *traditio*. Our contemporary meaning for the term in English and other modern European languages preserves the general sense of handing over, or passing on, something to someone else.

The action of transferring or transmitting gives us clues to the various factors that play roles in tradition. These factors may be gathered into at least six different categories, which are seldom identified at all and, to my knowledge, have never been identified clearly in any one place. The first of these categories comprises persons who play particular roles in tradition. At least six of these can be easily singled out: initiator, establisher, transmitter, receiver, enactor, and bearer.[37] Each of these can be one or more persons, but for the sake of simplicity and economy, I refer to them in the singular. The initiator of a tradition is a person who begins the tradition. The establisher consists of whoever sets it on firm ground. The transmitter is the person who passes the tradition to someone else. The receiver is someone who accepts the tradition. The enactor is the person who carries out, or engages in carrying out, the tradition. And the bearer of the tradition functions as its repository or keeper, that is, as "the bank" where the tradition is "deposited." These roles are not exclusive of each other. For example, the initiator of a tradition can also be a transmitter of it, a transmitter can also be a receiver and enactor, and all can be bearers and enactors.

The second category of factors that play important roles in tradition comprises different kinds of actions, six of which are pertinent: The action of initiating a tradition, the action of establishing it, the action of transmitting it, the action of receiving it, the action of enacting it, and the action of bearing it. Clearly, these six actions correspond to the different roles we saw persons play in tradition.

Very important, of course, is the content of tradition, which is also sometimes called the object of tradition. This content has been understood in many different ways. Among those frequently cited are beliefs, doctrines, acts, rituals, texts, things, rules, and institutions.[38]

The aims and uses of tradition can be numerous and, therefore, there is no point in trying to give even an approximate list of them. Suffice it to say that the aim of a tradition can be such different things as enlightenment, pleasure, identity formation or preservation, and domination. And, of course, these parallel the uses that can be made of traditions, for these can be, and are, used in a large number of ways.

As important as the factors mentioned is the means through which traditions are passed on. And here again the possibilities are many, for there are many ways in which a tradition may be transmitted. At least two of these are fundamental and frequent: A text or a showing. The first can describe a tradition and thus communicate it; the second reveals the tradition by presenting us with it. One can tell one's child about celebrating a birthday, or one can show her what such celebration is by pointing to it.

Finally, also important is the context, for this affects some of the factors mentioned. For example, certain historical circumstances can prompt the establishment of traditions that otherwise would not have been established at all. Celebrating Thanksgiving became established in the United States owing to very particular circumstances surrounding the Pilgrims and native Americans. These included a religious attitude, the availability of turkey, and so on. The same tradition was never established in Mexico, and the reason has to do precisely with particular circumstances in that country. Moreover, not only the establishment, but also the particular forms traditions take and the ways they are enacted are affected by context.

B. Conceptions of Tradition

It has been common to conceive tradition in terms of one or more of the factors I have listed. Of course, it would make no sense to identify some of them with it. The personal roles involved in tradition fall into this category, and the same can be said about the aim, uses, and context of tradition, as well as the actions of initiating, establishing, receiving, or bearing it. But at least four of the mentioned factors make sense *prima facie*: the action of transmission, the content of transmission, the means used in the transmission, and the action of enacting a tradition. All of these have had their explicit defenders, but more often than not, the view that tradition consists in one or more of these is merely assumed, or, if stated, no attempt is made to argue for it. Nor is it made clear why all four of these factors are identified with tradition or how they relate to each other. This state of affairs is particularly evident in theological contexts in which authors are often more interested in causing in an audience a kind of feeling, attitude, or even in some cases a certain non-rational enlightenment or vision, than in precise rational understanding.

These understandings of tradition are evident in dictionary entries. Of course, dictionaries are not concerned with the correct way of understanding terms, that is, with the formulation of concepts that are cogent and useful; they merely catalogue the uses of words, and these uses can be, and often are, conceptually confusing. *Malgré* what a few Oxford philosophers used to think some years back about the nature of philosophy, the philosopher's job is not to become a lexicographer. We do not merely catalogue the ways people speak; our task is rather to develop conceptual schemes that make sense of our experience and often determine that we should speak differently than we do. Contrary to Strawson's notorious claim, our business involves prescription, not mere description.[39]

Nonetheless, dictionaries are helpful in that they confirm some of the basic intuitions of the speakers of a language concerning the meaning of terms and thus the concepts to which they refer. Consider, for example, what the *Oxford English Dictionary* tells us under the entry on tradition.[40]

1. The action of handing over (something material) to another; delivery, transfer.

2. A giving up, surrender; betrayal.

3. Delivery, especially oral delivery, of information or instruction.

4. The action of transmitting or 'handing down,' or fact of being handed down, from one to another, or from generation to generation; transmission of statements, beliefs, rules, customs, or the like, especially by word of mouth or by practice without writing.

5. A. That which is thus handed down; a statement, belief, or practice transmitted (especially orally) from generation to generation.

B. More vaguely: A long established and generally accepted custom or method of procedure, having almost the force of a law; an immemorial usage; the body (or any one) of the

experiences and usages of any branch or school
of art or literature, handed down by predecessors
and generally followed.

This entry confirms for us three of the four understandings of tradition mentioned earlier as making
sense *prima facie*: tradition as an action of transmitting something, as the content of transmission, and
as enactment—the means of transmission is not
recorded. All the other ways of understanding it listed
in the *OED* are in fact reducible to these. (1)-(4) are
reducible to the first; (5A) is reducible to the second;
and (5B) is reducible to the second or the third. Now,
the question for us concerns the adequacy of these
conceptions of tradition. Unfortunately, we encounter difficulties with all four at the outset.

The difficulty with the identification of tradition
with the means of transmission concerns the fact that
the means used to transmit a tradition can be a text
or an action of ostension that calls attention to, and
reveals, the tradition. But neither of these appears to
be, strictly speaking, the tradition itself. The tradition
of eating turkey on Thanksgiving seems to be neither
a text that describes the action of eating turkey on
Thanksgiving nor an action used in order to bring
attention to it.

More promising is the action of transmission itself
insofar as this is suggested by the etymology of the
term and many authors explicitly speak of it as tradi-

tion.[41] However, this again does not appear to be correct, for in the action performed in transmission there seems to be more than one action and at least two different kinds of actions performed independently of each other. The action of eating turkey on Thanksgiving, for example, can be performed in solitude, and this does not detract from it qualifying as the enactment of the tradition. Moreover, it can be performed in front of people who know, and are engaged in carrying out, the tradition, and this seems to imply that no transmission has taken place. The reason is that for transmission to take place, when this is understood as passing something on to those who do not have it, there has to be someone else who is in principle capable of receiving what is transmitted, even if the person in question does not in fact receive it.

The enactment of a tradition again seems promising in that it is, after all, an instance of it. But precisely because it is an enactment of the tradition, it seems not to be the tradition itself. A celebration of Thanksgiving does not appear to be the tradition of celebrating Thanksgiving.

Finally, content appears quite promising as a candidate for tradition, for the content seems to be what: (1) the initiator of the tradition initiates, (2) the establisher establishes, (3) the transmitter passes on, (4) the receiver is supposed to receive, (5) the means of transmission is intended to convey, and (6) the bearer of the tradition keeps. Those who argue for this position, then, identify a tradition (*traditio*) with what is transferred (*traditum*).[42]

At least two difficulties may be raised, however, with this understanding of tradition. The first is an intuition: The *traditum* seems to be what is passed on in a tradition, not the tradition itself. And the second is that there are many *tradita* that do not seem to be traditions. Indeed, content can come in a great variety, as we saw earlier, so that if tradition is understood merely as a *traditum*, that is, as something handed down, then practically anything can be a tradition. This can include beliefs, actions, texts, things, buildings, rules, prayers, institutions, and practices, to mention just a few examples.[43] But most of these do not appear to be right, so one begins to wonder whether the view that tradition is simply content, that is, something transmitted, without further qualification is viable. Indeed, some of the items mentioned can be easily dismissed. Things are difficult to reconcile with a tradition: Does it make any sense to say that a piece of bread, a ball, or even a person is a tradition? Buildings fall into the same category and thus can also be eliminated. And institutions can be set aside because they can be analyzed in various ways which involve some of the other items on our list, such as rules and things.

In short, then, even the understanding of tradition in terms of the four ways that looked *prima facie* promising turns out to be problematic. Moreover, also problematic is that we have no clear way to favor one of these over the others or even to eliminate any of them altogether. The reason, I submit, is that we have not gone deep enough into the question of what a tradition is. In order to do this, we need to begin by identifying the general category to which traditions belong and then proceed, within that general category, to identify what distinguishes tradition from other members of it.

In this search, we get some guidance from the four understandings of tradition identified earlier: the action of transmission, the action of enactment, the content, and the means of transmission. One important thing to note about these is that all four can be actions. This is clear in the action of transmission and the action of enactment. But although not as clear, the content transmitted and the means of transmission can also be actions: the first because actions can be what is being transmitted, and the second because an action of ostension, for example, can be used as means of transmission. Moreover, two of these four can be texts: the content—as when one transmits a set of scriptures—and the means—as when one uses written or spoken language to tell about a tradition. Finally, the content can in principle be all sorts of things, but many of these do not in fact make sense or are reducible to others. I mentioned already some that do not make sense, but among those that are reducible to others are rules, prayers, and practices. Rules can be subsumed under the category of beliefs; practices fall into the category of action; and prayers fall into the categories of actions, beliefs, or texts. A practice is a repeated action, whether its repetition is motivated by a desire to get better at it, or just by custom. And a prayer can be: (1) an action or set of actions, as when someone engages in saying the "Lord's Prayer"; (2) a belief or set of beliefs one entertains when one says some words, again as in the "Lord's Prayer"; (3) a text of say, the "Lord's Prayer"; or (4) a combination of two or more of these.

So we end up with only two serious contenders for content, in addition to actions: texts and beliefs. But texts, as we shall see, are pertinent for tradition only when they express beliefs, so it turns out that there are only two serious candidates for the general category to which traditions belong: beliefs and actions. In the next chapter, I argue that the first does not work, and in the chapter that follows it, I present an understanding of tradition as action, adding further conditions that distinguish tradition within this category. For the sake of clarity, moreover, I also distinguish tradition from custom, habit, and disposition.

4
Tradition As Belief

In order to understand the view of tradition as belief
and to determine its viability, we need to begin by
presenting a working conception of belief. But this
is not easy, for belief is a highly contested notion.
Let me mention four of the most common conceptions of it:

(1) Beliefs are views expressed in propositions.

(2) Beliefs are views expressed in propositions that
are held by some person or persons to be true.

(3) Beliefs are views expressed in propositions that
are held by some persons or persons to be true, but
for which the person or persons in question do not
have sufficient evidence.

(4) Beliefs are certain kinds of texts, namely, linguistic formulations of beliefs when these are taken
in senses (1), (2), or (3).

An example of (1) is the proposition 'The world is
round.' An example of (2) is this same proposition
when held by some person to be true. A current
example of (3) is the proposition 'There exists extra-
terrestrial life in the universe' provided it is held by
someone to be true, because there is still insufficient
evidence that there is life outside the Earth. Of
course, in case sufficient evidence were produced in
support of the proposition, holding it would cease
to be a belief in this sense. On the other hand, if

the evidence were sufficient to show the proposition false, then holding the proposition would still be a belief, although a clearly false one. An example of (4) is the English sentence 'The world is round.' Position (4) can be unpacked into (1), (2), or (3), but to do so would be both tiresome and unnecessary, for which reason I dispense with it.

Four views of tradition, corresponding to these four views of belief, are common.[44] Those who speak of tradition often understand it in these ways, as when they refer to:

> The Catholic Tradition
> The Jewish Tradition
> The American Tradition
> The Aristotelian Tradition
> The Empiricist (or Empirical) Tradition

When Roman Catholic theologians speak of the Catholic Tradition, for example, they often have in mind a collection of doctrines which goes back to Christ and the Apostles, to the body of texts that contains these doctrines, or to both. The Jewish Tradition consists of a body of regulations claimed to have originated with Moses, the texts that express them, or both. The American Tradition involves a set of views understood in the mentioned ways. To speak of the Aristotelian Tradition in philosophy sometimes means that one is speaking about certain texts which in some ways are related to Aristotle, at

other times about certain principles or views which
are claimed to be inspired by Aristotle's doctrines or
those of his followers, and sometimes about both.
In all cases, it appears that tradition is taken as a set
of beliefs when these are understood in one or more
of the four mentioned ways.

Now, if tradition is going to serve to explain communication and the transmission of knowledge on
the one hand, and group identity on the other, it is
clear that it needs to function as a bridge and this
in turn requires both that it be commonly accessible
and that it retain its identity through time. However,
when tradition is understood exclusively as belief, it
appears that it can do neither.

A. The Problem of Common Accessibility

The problem of common accessibility has to do
with the Hermeneutic Circle. For if belief is understood in any of the four ways mentioned, it does not
appear possible for tradition to be commonly accessible. Indeed, we can dispose of this matter rather
quickly, insofar as tradition refers to something to
which we have no common access except when we
understand it as a text, and if we understand tradition
as a text, then we are back in the circle of language.
Whether tradition is taken as a view, a view held,
or a view held without sufficient evidence, we are
speaking about propositions, and the only access
we have to propositions, except for the ones we
entertain ourselves, is through language. Indeed,

some philosophers would argue that even those propositions we entertain ourselves are mediated by language, but this is a very strong claim which I do not need (nor wish) to defend for my argument to hold. For present purposes, it is sufficient to point out that, in order to communicate these views—that is, these propositions—to others, we need to put them into words. But if we do this, then tradition becomes a text, which is indeed what many contemporary philosophers claim.[45] Reducing tradition to texts, however, opens the door to the Hermeneutic Circle.

B. The Problem of Identity

The problem of identity comes up when tradition is taken as belief for the following reason: In order for tradition to serve as a bridge for communication, the transmission of knowledge, and group identity, it has itself to accommodate continuity within discontinuity. But it cannot do so as long as it is conceived as belief, so the problem of continuity vs. discontinuity becomes insurmountable. This is clear when one considers two extreme and opposed views with respect to this issue, for they reveal the underlying assumptions and problems that create the difficulty. I call these the Heraclitean and the Parmenidean views, and I take them up next in order to show how their conception of tradition as belief lies at the heart of their difficulties.

1. Heraclitean View

Those who favor the Heraclitean view argue that, although one may speak of the identity of traditions through time, traditions in fact are in constant flux, so their identity cannot be conceived in terms of common features as it was proposed in the last chapter, whether as absolute, relative, or the identity of similarity.[46] Rather, the identity of tradition needs to be conceived as what I called pseudo-identity in chapter 2, for the diachronic identity of traditions is founded merely on temporal continuity. So, for example, that tradition A at t_1 and tradition B at t_2 are the same means merely that there is temporal continuity between them, that is, that the temporal location of A and B is not mediated by any other temporal location, say t_3.

Now, if we understand tradition as a set of beliefs (in any one of the four ways listed earlier) and we adopt the Heraclitean position, then it is clear that the beliefs that constitute a tradition can be quite different, and indeed even contradictory, from time to time, for they need not have anything in common. One could argue, for example, that what Roman Catholics believe today and what they believed 500 years ago are actually quite different things, although the Catholic Tradition preserves its diachronic identity insofar as there has been temporal continuity between the beliefs of Roman Catholics throughout the 500 years in question.

Some might regard this consequence of the Heraclitean view as an advantage in the context of religion, for it allows progression and evolution in religious doctrine. Indeed, the position is quite appealing to those who wish, as Karl Barth did, to preserve openness and freedom and to allow maximum room for accommodating the needs of the present and the future. If a tradition is not in any way fixed, then it can remain open to whatever processes of change the community deems to be required to meet new challenges in their lives. Consider for example certain religious doctrines, such as the creation of the world by God in six days. The belief in this story is part of the Roman Catholic Tradition. Now, if we adopt a Heraclitean view, this story is open to interpretation, thus accommodating quite different views about what it means exactly. It does not matter that the persons who heard it when it was first composed believed that it meant literally that God created the world in six days and that Roman Catholics living today do not, for the tradition derives its identity from temporal continuity rather than propositional content.

The paradox in this view is that, in principle, it would be possible for the beliefs in a particular tradition to become just the opposite of what they are. Roman Catholics could in principle come to believe as part of their tradition that God is not one substance and three persons, or any other belief that is contrary to some other belief Roman Catholics held at some other time in the history of their faith.

In short, this position makes room for change and evolution in tradition but at the price of making it impossible to account for its diachronic identity in any but an accidental and contingent manner. And this in turn makes it impossible for this view of tradition to help solve the problems of communication, the transmission of knowledge, and group identity.

2. Parmenidean View

The Parmenidean view argues that the identity of tradition has to be taken strictly, in terms of a complete commonality of features, that is, as what I called absolute identity in chapter 2. For tradition A to be identical to tradition B, it is required that nothing in A be different from what it is in B, and vice versa.

Applying this position to tradition understood as a set of beliefs, we get the view that the set of propositions or texts that constitute a tradition must be exactly the same throughout the existence of the tradition. If there is a Catholic Tradition, the beliefs which constitute this tradition must be exactly the same at every point of its history. This means that Christ's Apostles and a Roman Catholic today must hold the same beliefs, if they are to be regarded as adhering to the same tradition.

Clearly, the strength of this position is that it can provide a strong conception of diachronic identity, and, thus, it is well poised to solve the puzzles of communication, knowledge, and group identity. On the other hand, the problem with it is that it does not appear to accommodate the kind of change that is evident in our experience of traditions. Indeed, the very language of traditions and the concepts in terms of which they are framed often differ in important ways throughout their history. For example, it would be hard to claim that the understanding of creation the authors of Genesis had is exactly the same as the understanding a Roman Catholic scientist has of it today. Consider again the so-called days in which the creative process took place. Today, this is taken figuratively by most Catholics to mean periods of millions of years in which the world evolved to its present form. But such a notion would have been beyond the understanding of a resident of the Arabian peninsula several thousand years ago. And consider the doctrine of the Trinity as framed in the Greek philosophical language of the Hellenistic period. Can we really take seriously that Christ's Apostles, most of whom were uneducated, understood this language? Nor does it say anywhere in the Christian Scriptures that spiritual wisdom brings with it gifts of technical knowledge about Greek philosophy. So one might claim with some reason that it makes no sense to hold that there has been no change in the beliefs regarded as part of the Roman Catholic Tradition. Of course, one could say that there is no change in the fundamental or canonical texts that

constitute it, but even if this were true—which it is
not—this is certainly not helpful when it comes to
the Hermeneutic Circle.

The Parmenidean understanding of tradition has
the advantage that it clearly preserves the diachronic
identity of the beliefs in question. The story of Genesis is to be held in the same way when it was written
and today. But even this is not uncontroversial, for
assuming that the doctrines believed at various times
as part of a tradition may be the same, there is still
the question of their interpretation. Consider the
fundamental Christian doctrine of the Trinity. Even
if one were to assume that there is only one valid formulation of this doctrine, is it not a fact that there are
many interpretations of it—perhaps as many as there
are theologians who discuss it? And I am not talking
about unorthodox ones—I am speaking about orthodox interpretations. One need only read Augustine,
Thomas Aquinas, and Francisco Suárez—to name
just three of the most influential orthodox Roman
Catholic theologians who have discussed the Trinity—to see that there are important differences in
the understanding of the doctrine. And if this is so
in the cases of such sophisticated thinkers, what can
we make of ordinary people? Does it make sense to
hold that everyone who adheres to a tradition has the
same views, that is, entertains the same propositions?
Indeed, this seems to be a very good reason to reject
the conception of tradition as a set of beliefs.

If we leave theology and move to philosophy, the difficulties with the Parmenidean view are even more clear: it does not properly account for our experience of philosophical traditions in that these change over time and very little, if anything, remains unmodified in them. Aristotle, Hegel, and Kant would all be shocked if they read some of the subsequent philosophers who claim to be members of the philosophical traditions to which they are supposed to have given birth. Indeed, consider the case of Aristotle and Thomas Aquinas. If there has ever been a true Aristotelian, Thomas was one. Yet, the Christian view of God he used to understand Aristotle's Unmoved Mover would have shocked Aristotle. And the centerpiece of Thomas' thought, his understanding of being as an act which perfects even essence, would have been unintelligible to the Stagirite.

In short, this conception of tradition preserves identity, but at a very high cost. For this reason, it is unacceptable.

C. Source of the Difficulties

The difficulties that plague the conception of tradition as belief have to do with common accessibility and identity. The first concerns the fact that, as we saw earlier, if tradition is conceived as belief, then it turns out to be nothing other than a set of propositions or of sentences that express those propositions. But the common accessibility of propositions is only through sentences, and sentences by themselves are incapable of revealing propositions and thus of defeating the Hermeneutic Circle. This is a sufficient reason to abandon the view of tradition as belief. But there is more, for the analysis of Heracliteanism and Parmenideanism shows a second area of weakness in the conception of tradition as belief.

Although Heracliteanism and Parmenideanism have not been described in the literature precisely in the way I have done it here, many authors have noticed the tension between continuity and discontinuity in tradition, between the old and the new, and the difficulty of accounting for its diachronic identity. And some have expressed dissatisfaction with solutions that seem to take into account only one of these alternatives. Indeed, some authors have said that it is the tension between the two, the desire to preserve the past and to make room for the present and the future, that characterizes the Western tradition.[47] Or, as one recent philosopher has put it in the context of religion in general, and particularly of Christian theology, it is the "tension between those whose primary concern is to safeguard the tradition—to ensure that no element of truth in it is lost—and those who want above all to do full justice to modern discoveries and contemporary experience."[48]

The dilemma faced by those who adopt either the Heraclitean or the Parmenidean view defies escape. The conception of tradition in a Heraclitean fashion makes room for the present and the future, allowing for change in accordance with new discoveries and needs, but then any kind of continuity with the past other than a temporal one is lost. And the conception of tradition in a Parmenidean way ensures a strong continuity with the past, but at the cost of not making room for the present or the future and the discoveries and experiences that these bring with them.

One way to deal with these dilemmas is to try to escape them through a middle ground between the extremes of Heracliteanism and Parmenideanism, but this is by no means easy. The reason is that the source of the difficulty underlying the problems of these two positions is to a great extent their common conception of tradition as belief. They both conceive tradition exclusively as a set of propositions or their linguistic expression, and once this is done, one is locked into the dialectic I have indicated, for it is not easy to account for the identity of tradition through time. Propositions and the sentences that express them seem to be either absolutely identical, as the Parmenideans hold, or to have only a pseudo-identity, as the Heracliteans maintain. Consider, for example, the proposition, 'God is one substance and three persons.' What modification of this proposition can be consistent with the preservation of its identity? Naturally, if we talk of a sentence instead of a proposition, then modifications are possible as long as the changes do not alter the meaning, that is, the proposition which the sentence expresses.[49] But the proposition itself seems to be incapable of modification without loss of identity.

My proposal in the face of these difficulties is to abandon the view of tradition as belief and adopt instead a view of it as action. This is the general category to which traditions belong. In order to claim any credibility for this view, however, I must also make clear the further conditions that traditions must satisfy and which distinguish traditions from other kinds of actions. This is the task of the next chapter.

5
Tradition As Action

It is useful to begin the investigation of the view of tradition as action by considering some very ordinary examples of traditions. The following should suffice initially:

Eating turkey on Thanksgiving
Celebrating birthdays
Observing Passover
Saying a prayer for the dead
Exchanging gifts on Christmas day

There is no question that all these are traditions: We call them traditions; we think of them as traditions; and no one would question us if we said they are traditions.

These examples share certain important characteristics. Most obvious is that they consist of certain kinds of actions. Clearly, not every kind of action qualifies as a tradition. Brushing my teeth is not a tradition, putting on the breaks when I am driving and a dog crosses the street in front of my car is not a tradition, and taking off my shoes when I am at the beach and I want to walk barefooted on the sand is not a tradition. Indeed, most actions in which we engage are not traditions, and if someone were to call them traditions, we would find it odd. We might think that the person who called them so either did not know what a tradition is—as say, a

very small child does not—or might not understand
English—as happens with some foreigners. It is clear,
then, that not all actions in which we engage qualify
as traditions. In fact, most actions are not traditions;
only certain kinds of actions are traditions.

This leads logically to a question: Is it just in virtue
of its kind that an action becomes a tradition? Is it
merely the action of eating turkey on Thanksgiving
that is sufficient to make of this action a tradition?
Surely not. A Cuban may happen to eat turkey on
Thanksgiving and that does not make her action a
tradition. She may not know the date; she may know
the date and not know that the date coincides with
Thanksgiving; she may know both the date and that
Americans regard this date as Thanksgiving Day, but
this may lack significance for her; and so on. In all
these cases, she eats turkey, but eating turkey for her
is not the enactment of a tradition.

Clearly, the kind to which an action belongs is not
what makes it a tradition, for traditions can consist
in very different kinds of actions. In the examples
given above, we have five different kinds of actions,
and they do not seem to share any property *qua* the
kinds of actions they are. Eating turkey, celebrating
birthdays, observing a holiday, saying a prayer, and
exchanging gifts are surely very different. In the first,
we are masticating and swallowing a certain kind of
food; in the second, we are having a party; in the
third, we are remembering a religious occasion; in
the fourth, we are addressing a divinity; and in the

last, we are giving and receiving gifts. In short, it does not seem to be characteristic of traditions that they involve any specific kind of action or even a generic kind of action. Many different kinds of actions can become traditions. To eating, celebrating, observing, praying, and exchanging, many other kinds of actions could be added, such as killing, drinking, copulating, sacrificing, speaking, and bowing.

Not every kind of action, however, can become a tradition, since certain kinds of actions cannot qualify under any circumstances. For example, a nervous tick which makes me blink repeatedly, digesting food, an emotive outburst, gasping for air when I am suffocating, seeing when I have my eyes open, and understanding what I read, cannot become traditions. Why? Because they are involuntary and unintentional, for these are the only significant features all these have in common. It appears that traditions are required to be both voluntary and intentional. So, we do after all have some features that must characterize actions that can become traditions, although these features are not specifically related to the kinds of action in question. We have now established some conditions of traditions: They are actions and they are both voluntary and intentional. We have also established that in principle any kind of voluntary and intentional action can become a tradition. But this is not enough to explain when an action does in fact become a tradition, for many voluntary and intentional actions never become traditions. For example, my eating fish last night was both voluntary and intentional, and yet it is not, and has not become, a tradition.

So far I have been speaking of actions in general or of kinds of actions rather than of individual and non-individual actions. The difference between individual and non-individual actions, however, is important, as will become evident later. The most common term to refer to non-individual actions is "universal actions." The notion of kind is not equivalent to that of universal, although sometimes it is confused with it. To talk about a kind is to speak about the species to which something belongs, in the same way I speak of species of mammals, for example. Universal contrasts with individual. The difference between an individual and a universal is that the first is a non-instantiable instance of the second, and therefore that the second is capable of instantiation.[50] Cat is universal because it is instantiable into this or that cat, whereas Peanut and Hunter (my two cats) are individual because they are non-instantiable instances of cat. Now, this can be applied to actions as well. The action of scratching one's head is universal because it can be instantiated in my action of scratching my head or your action of scratching yours. For the understanding of tradition, the distinction between universal and individual actions is important, as I shall explain presently.

Before I do so, however, I need to add that philosophers disagree strongly as to whether universals exist and about the sort of existence they have. This issue is usually known as the problem of universals.[51] Indeed, although this may appear absurd to an ordinary person, some philosophers have even doubted the existence of individuals. I have no space here to deal with this matter, so I adopt a view I have defended elsewhere.[52] According to it, only individuals can be said to exist or not exist, and it is a category mistake to talk about universals as existing or not existing.

For our present purposes, this means that only non-instantiable instances of universal actions—such as my action of scratching my head—exist or do not exist, and talking about the existence or non-existence of universal actions—such as the action of scratching's one's head—makes no sense. It is for this reason that traditions are initiated and established through individual actions and exist only through them, for the categories of existence and non-existence do not apply to universals. The tradition of eating turkey on Thanksgiving, say, exists only in the individual actions that instantiate it, that is, my eating turkey two Thanksgivings ago, your eating turkey last Thanksgiving, and so on.

What has been said makes it possible to explain the distinction between living and dead traditions. A living tradition is an action with instances in the present, whereas a dead tradition, on the other hand, has instances only in the past. Eating turkey on Thanksgiving is a living tradition in the United

States; giving gifts to children on the Christian feast of the Epiphany is a living, but threatened, tradition in some Hispanic countries; and the divinization of dead Roman emperors is a dead tradition. Of course, 'present' here cannot be understood as meaning "now," for it is clear that we are not celebrating Thanksgiving by eating turkey today, say, February 23, 2003, and yet this is a living tradition. 'Present' must refer to the fact that, were Thanksgiving today, we would be celebrating it by eating turkey. But even this is too strong, for it is possible that, for many reasons—such as an epidemic that killed all the turkeys, an allergy to turkeys developed by the population, and so on—no American will eat turkey on not just one, but many, Thanksgivings. I shall return to this shortly.

Dead and past traditions are extensionally equivalent, although the terms through which we refer to them are not intensionally equivalent. Future traditions have instances only in the future. This means that they occur always in the future relative to some particular point in time. Merely possible traditions could have instances in principle but never actually do. Actual and living traditions are extensionally equivalent, even though the terms through which we refer to them have different intensions. Actual traditions "exist," whereas living traditions are "alive." The notions of actuality and life are not the same, but they are often used as such in ordinary speech.

Living, of course, is a metaphor but nonetheless quite effective for understanding what is involved here.

One more point needs to be made clear with respect to living traditions because, as I already mentioned, the actions that constitute living traditions are not permanently instantiated. If this is so, then where do traditions exist while they are not being enacted?

To say that a tradition exists in the awareness of those who from time to time enact it will not suffice because humans are not constantly and permanently aware of anything. They go to sleep, for example. Only God, as conceived in the Jewish and Christian religions, for example, could be said to be constantly and permanently aware of anything. But God's case is not useful for our account insofar as traditions are human phenomena, even if some religions believe some of them have been initiated by God. So, where do living traditions exist when they are not being enacted?

They do exist, as dispositions, in those human beings who accept them, even though strictly speaking they are not dispositions themselves. Dispositions incline us to behave in certain ways when the circumstances call for it; a disposition affects the way we think and act. Dispositions are a contentious subject of discussion in contemporary philosophy, but for our present purposes we need not get into the details of this controversy.[53] Suffice it to say that dispositions incline those who have them to act in certain ways, so they can be described by conditionals that tell us how the subject (or object) in question would behave in particular situations. I have a disposition to drink red wine if, whenever I am given the choice between red and white, I tend to choose red. Likewise, there is a disposition to eat turkey in most Americans when Thanksgiving comes around, because they tend to do so.

Dispositions are not memories of past events. The memory I have of celebrating Thanksgiving last year is not my disposition to celebrate Thanksgiving, for it is both particular and directed toward the past. Rather, dispositions are features of our minds that incline us to do certain things in the future, that is, they are actually existing mental qualities that characterize those who have them, predisposing them to engage in certain actions under appropriate circumstances. Perhaps even the word 'quality' is misplaced here, for the acquisition of a disposition entails rather a structural change in our minds that affects the way we act.[54] But a disposition is not something inevitable, like seeing a pink world whenever we look through pink-tinted glasses. A disposition is like a path or rut in which we tend to fall whenever we find ourselves in certain situations, and which we have difficulty resisting even when we consciously try, although we can in fact resist it if we will to do so. But dispositions should not be confused with actions and therefore with traditions. A disposition to eat at certain times of the day is not the action of eating, but rather the mental structure that inclines those who have it to eat at such times.[55]

The living tradition of eating turkey on Thanksgiving exists as a tendency in the mind of most Americans to eat turkey on Thanksgiving. Americans do not need to be eating turkey all the time in order for the tradition to be alive. Indeed, this would not make sense, for it would be impossible in that the tradition applies only once a year; the rest of the time we merely have the mental disposition to eat turkey when Thanksgiving comes around. The fact that we are speaking of a disposition explains something else about living traditions, namely, that it is not necessary for the tradition that it be enacted every time the appropriate circumstances occur. It is altogether possible that some Americans may not eat turkey on a particular Thanksgiving—indeed many do not, either because they do not like turkey, or because they have no money to buy a turkey, or for some other contingent reason, as mentioned earlier. And it is also possible, although unlikely, that no American will eat turkey on a particular Thanksgiving day or perhaps even on several Thanksgiving days. This could happen if there were an epidemic that killed all turkeys, for example. For a tradition to be alive it is only necessary that, other things being equal, the members of the group who bear the tradition have the disposition to enact it.

The reference to living traditions brings us to another condition that traditions must satisfy. A

tradition cannot be instantiated just once. In order
for eating turkey on Thanksgiving to be a tradition,
it must be instantiated more than once. This is a
tradition in part because it is instantiated every year.
And even if the tradition stopped, eating turkey on
Thanksgiving would still be a tradition, although it
would be a dead one, for there have been enough
instantiations of it to make it a tradition.

But is there a minimum number of instantiations
under which a kind of action is not a tradition, and
over which it is? Clearly, many instantiations will
do, but what if the instantiations are few? Consider
the hypothetical case in which the Pilgrims started
eating turkey on Thanksgiving and did it for a few
years but then stopped. Would eating turkey on
Thanksgiving be a tradition, then? I do not see why
not, although obviously it would be a dead tradition rather than a living one today, and its bearers
would not be Americans, but the Pilgrims. Under
these conditions we could say that this tradition was
short-lived, although still a tradition.

Now let us consider a case in which the action
is enacted only twice. Would this be a tradition?
I tend to think that the answer is yes, although
ultimately the correct answer would depend on the
circumstances. Consider the following example. A
few years ago, I decided that every Christmas Eve I
would have a wine-tasting party for my daughters
and my sons-in-law. I bought half-a-dozen bottles
of wine, ranging from the very cheap to the very

expensive. The idea was that each couple would taste the wines, blindly of course, and that each couple would get a case of the wine they liked best. Of course, they all loved the idea and I repeated the affair the following year, at which time Clarisa, my youngest daughter, referred to this event as "one of our family traditions." (By the way, this tradition has cost me more than expected, for it has turned out that the taste in wine of my children and their husbands is rather expensive.) In her mind, this had become something traditional for us to do on that day, but it was something for our immediate family only. Indeed, a grandnephew of mine was spending Christmas with us at the time and he wanted very much to participate. However, although he was allowed to taste and drink the wine and participate in that sense, he was not an official participant, that is, his choice of a wine would not result in his receiving a case of it. Everyone understood this. The tradition extended only to our immediate family.

The point of this example is that tasting different wines on Christmas Eve and all the accompanying actions became a family tradition after it was repeated just once. Of course, when I die, perhaps the tradition will end, although it is possible that my wife would continue it. Or perhaps it will be dormant until one of my daughters or sons-in-law revives it, when his or her own children are of an appropriate age. And I am quite sure that, if the tradition were to be continued by my wife after my death, everyone would refer to it as having been initiated by me; and if the tradition were discontinued for a while, when revived, the ones involved would speak of "its revival."

This example further reveals four other important points for our investigation. First, traditions may become dormant and be revived at later times; second, they can be initiated, and even invented, by individuals; third, they are social rather than personal affairs; and four, they have historical origins. These points are quite consistent with the common-sense view of tradition most of us have. Particularly important is that traditions do not pertain to individual persons, but rather to groups. For example, the celebration of a birthday in the United States involves blowing out the candles of a cake by the person whose birthday is being celebrated, eating the cake by those present at the celebration, singing Happy Birthday by persons in attendance except for the one whose birthday it is, and so on. Everyone in the group participates in some way by engaging in the overall festivity and this is done by carrying out some action, but the particular actions in which they engage do not all have to be of the same kind. There is one overall action, namely, celebrating a birthday; although this action breaks down into various specific ones, such as blowing out the candles, singing Happy Birthday, and eating cake. Clearly, I cannot establish a tradition for just myself. Indeed, I cannot even initiate one; traditions are eminently social affairs. And this applies even when the action involves only one human being. For example, there might be a tradition to say a prayer on a certain date or at a certain hour, and this might involve only individual persons, but the tradition is still social in that it applies to all members of a group, or if it applies only to some members of it, it applies to them *qua* members of the group. The tradition is not a matter of individual practice.

The social character of traditions can be easily illustrated by comparing traditions and habits. The locus of the latter are individual persons who have acquired them after appropriate repetitions of certain actions.[56] This means that a habit may be had by a single person and no one else. There are good and bad habits. We often call good habits virtues and bad habits vices. Drinking excessively is a bad habit, and drinking in moderation is a good one, but in both cases, the habit belongs to an individual person and pertains to her alone, even if it may affect others as well. By contrast, the locus of traditions are groups of people. Of course, the bearers and enactors are individual persons, but there must be, or must have been, more than one person who bears and enacts the tradition and these persons must be tied in more than artificial or accidental ways. Traditions pertain to constituted groups.

Traditions, then, are social phenomena and do not pertain to individual persons in the sense that I, as an individual person, cannot have traditions.

I may have habits, or routines, or dispositions, or I may engage in certain activities at certain times. I may even pass on to myself views and beliefs at different times. For example, I may formulate some idea and write it down. Then I may forget all about it and later find what I wrote and be reminded of the idea. So, one may ask: How is this different from what happens when someone transmits something to us from the past? One could be tempted to argue, then, that individual persons can have traditions. But this is a mistake, for traditions transcend the lives of such persons. Tasting of wines on Christmas Eve for our family, eating turkey on Thanksgiving for Americans, and making the sign of the cross on certain occasions for Roman Catholics are all group events even if they are enacted by individual persons. The traditions apply to persons *qua* members of a group, even though it is individuals who carry out the actions. Indeed, this is so even in cases in which there is only one member of the group who enacts the tradition because he or she is alone, or even if he or she is the only one who can do so because he or she is the only one who survives.

The social aspect of traditions has at least one other important dimension of which we should take note here: Traditions are established by groups rather than individual persons. I cannot decide that this or that will be a tradition, even if in fact I am the initiator of the tradition in the sense that I am the first who thinks of, and engages in, the acts that are subsequently adopted by a group as a tradition. Traditions may be initiated by individual persons, but not established by them. Consider the example of the family tradition mentioned earlier concerning the tasting and selecting of wines on Christmas Eve. The idea for the procedure was mine, and I was also responsible for putting the idea into practice the first time. This means clearly that I initiated the tradition. However, it was not I who decided that this was to become a family tradition, that is, to establish it. Indeed, it is not clear that any one person in particular did. Clarisa certainly noticed that this procedure had become a family tradition, but surely it was neither she nor her saying so that established it as such. She considered herself merely someone who put into words something that was already a reality. Interestingly, when she made her remark, no one challenged it. The group merely accepted, or perhaps realized for the first time, that a tradition had been established. Now, clearly every one would regard me as the initiator of the tradition, but it was not I who established the tradition. In order for a kind of action to become a tradition it must be accepted by the group.

The view that traditions are established by groups rather than individual persons should not undermine the fact that traditions can be initiated and even invented by individual persons, as the example of the wine-tasting on Christmas Eve shows. Indeed, the view that traditions are inventions is common these

days, being part of the general tendency to speak of
social realities as inventions.[57] Now, it is not clear
that by 'invented' the same thing is always meant. In
one sense, one can say that traditions are invented,
and even invented by individual persons if one means
something like what I did when I first thought of
the procedure I initiated in my family for Christmas
Eve. But there is also another sense of 'invention' in
which what is meant is that traditions are fictions put
together in order to provide unity and cohesion for
a group, for example. This is what happens, according to some political scientists, when traditions are
used in the context of nationalism. These cases are
different from the case of the wine-tasting affair in
that the latter procedure was initiated by me and then
repeated without the original intention of establishing a tradition. But in some cases, one may wish to
argue that a person or persons initiate a procedure
precisely with the intention that it should become a
tradition, and this then justifies calling it an invention, but in a different sense from that employed
in the example of the wine.[58] Of course, such an
intention is not sufficient to establish the tradition,
for ultimately the group must consent to it, and as it
were appropriate it, before the procedure in question
becomes a tradition. Nonetheless, we cannot ignore
the fact that the procedure is intended as a tradition
from the start. Such traditions as singing a national
anthem on certain occasions or, in the United States,

saying the Pledge of Allegiance on other occasions are traditions of this sort.

That traditions are social phenomena having to do with groups of people does not entail that just any group of persons can become the locus of a tradition. Certainly not if the group is an arbitrary or accidental gathering. To pick several persons at random and make an aggregate of them is not enough for the group to serve as the locus of a tradition. And the same applies to an accidental gathering, such as the people who happen to be traveling on a plane, eating at a restaurant, or swimming in a river, at some particular time. One reason why these groups of persons cannot serve as the loci of traditions is that, as arbitrarily selected groups or accidental conglomerates, they do not have anything that binds the members of the groups together other than external factors, such as the will of the one who selects the members or a spatio-temporal location. Traditions require both some stability and the possibility of greater stability, because the instantiations of traditions occur over time. Diachronicity is essential to traditions. A synchronic tradition makes no sense. If all instantiations of a tradition occurred at the same time, there would be no tradition. This is one of the few important things suggested by the etymology of the term—the notion of passing something on requires diachronicity, that is, successive instantiations.

The diachronicity required by traditions is possible in social groups, such as families, nations, ethnic groups, religious communities, cities, professional organizations, institutions of various sorts, social clubs, and so on. Particular examples are the Gracia family, the Argentinian nation, Hispanics, the Roman Catholic Church, Milwaukee, the American Philosophical Association, Marquette University, the Rotary Club, and so on. The members of all these are related in important ways that unite them and provide the stability required for traditions to take hold and flourish.

Some of these groups, such as ethnic ones, pose particular problems insofar as they do not appear to share properties throughout their existence. For example, there is nothing that appears to be common to all Hispanics throughout their history, even though at different times and places some, or all, have shared some properties.[59] Under these conditions, then, does it make sense to speak of ethnic traditions, that is, traditions whose loci are ethnic groups? Can we speak of Hispanic traditions, Jewish traditions, and so on?

It would be odd to say that it does not, for we often speak of these groups as having traditions, and, in fact, many of the traditions to which we more frequently refer are ethnic. Of course, one way to deny this is to say that, because ethnic and national groups often coincide extensionally, we tend to think of ethnic traditions when in fact the traditions in question are national. We might be thinking about Cuban traditions as ethnic when in fact they are national. This might be true in some cases, but it does not seem right in all of them. Consider the case of Hispanic traditions. There is no Hispanic nation, so if we speak of traditions whose locus is the group of people we know as Hispanics, we must be speaking of ethnic traditions. But, returning to the difficulty we initially raised, how can there be Hispanic traditions if Hispanics have no common properties at all times and places?

The answer is in part that, as we shall see later, traditions themselves evolve. For the existence of Hispanic traditions, it is not required that there be something common to all Hispanics throughout time. And in part the answer is that most ethnic traditions, like the properties of ethnic groups, have a limited duration. So there can be long-lived Hispanic traditions that change and relatively short-lived traditions that may not change throughout their duration. It would be misleading to speak of *the* Hispanic tradition as if there were only one such tradition for Hispanics.

So much for traditions and ethnic groups, but what about racial groups? Can we make sense of racial traditions? Can we speak of White and Black traditions? Do Whites and Blacks have traditions, *qua* Whites and Blacks? It all depends on what is meant by a race. If a race is considered ethnically, as they often are, then what has been said about ethnic groups and traditions also applies to them.[60] On the other hand, if races are conceived as involving physical properties passed on genetically, then it would make as little sense to speak of racial traditions as of traditions whose loci would be blond people, or blue-eyed people, or blind people, or handicapped people, and so on.[61] And I do not think we can make sense of these. In short, we must reject the idea of racial traditions, unless what we mean by races are ethnic groups.

Finally, the example of the wine tasting on Christmas Eve also makes clear that traditions have a historical origin. It was on a certain Christmas Eve that the first enactment of the tradition I initiated in my family took place. This is important because it serves to distinguish traditions that could be the same in content from each other. Someone else might have started the same kind of tradition elsewhere at a different time, but that could never be the same as the tradition I initiated, because they would have different historical origins.

There is still one more factor in tradition that needs to be brought out before we can arrive at an adequate conception of it. For, even putting together everything that has been said, I have still not sufficiently narrowed down the conditions under which certain kinds of actions become traditions. One way to bring this last factor into the open is by comparing traditions and social customs, for it is clear that many social customs satisfy the conditions I have so far indicated and yet they are not traditions.[62] Consider table manners. To hold the fork with the left hand, to say "please" when one wishes for someone to pass the salt, for a male to pull out a chair for a female, and so on, are all customary in certain societies, and yet they are not considered traditions. These actions are multiply and diachronically instantiated and their loci are social groups. Indeed, earlier on I referred to some of these as traditions or as traditional behavior, and in fact we often say things like: "It is traditional for males to pull chairs out for females." So there is clearly a broad sense in which these are considered traditions or traditional. However, I believe that 'tradition' and 'traditional' in these cases are used as synonyms for 'custom' and 'customary' and thus do not in fact capture the more precise sense of 'tradition' with which I am concerned here. So, how can we distinguish mere social customs from traditions when these are conceived strictly?

I submit that traditions properly speaking can be distinguished from customs in terms of three factors: (1) the intention of re-enactment among those who enact them; (2) the significance that traditions have for the identity of the group which is its locus; and (3) the awareness of that significance on the part of the members of the group. From the examples of traditions cited, it is clear that the enactment of a certain kind of action is not enough for an action to constitute a tradition. There has to be re-enactment and this must be accompanied by an intention to do so. The tradition of wine-tasting on Christmas Eve requires not only the re-enactment of wine-tasting, but also the intention to do so. This is something missing in mere customs. In many customs we repeat certain actions with the intention to enact them, but without the intention to repeat them. When I hold the fork with my left hand I intend to do so, but I do not intend to repeat an action carried out by others before me.

But this is not all. The significance of the re-enactment for the identity of the group and the awareness of it are also essential for tradition, and not required in customs. Social groups, unlike groups based on common physical properties (e.g., people with brown eyes), are tied through complex social relations that help unite them and establish their identity. Eliminate these relations and the group loses its unity as a group. This explains the significance of traditions and the importance of the awareness of such significance on the part of the members of the group.[63]

Consider the case of a nation. This is a group of people united by a common bond of will to abide by a system of laws.[64] This system determines the conditions of belonging to the group, regulates the relations among the members of the group, separates the group from other groups, and preserves the group's internal unity. But the law is a very dry affair; it has to do with actions that are allowed, actions that are required, and actions that are forbidden. As such, it is not enough to provide group unity and grounds for the members of the group to identify with the group. There has to be an element of inspiration and solidarity in order for the members of a group to acquiesce to a system of laws and to identify with each other. This is provided by traditions and symbols. Symbols, such as a flag or a national anthem, stand for the unity and identity of the group; traditions are certain activities that help locate and use these symbols in the lives of the citizens. Singing the Star-Spangled Banner on certain occasions, flying the Stars and Stripes in certain places, saying the Pledge of Allegiance at particular ceremonies, and so on, are all traditions that emphasize the symbols of unity of the American nation. They are all significant for national identity and regarded as such.[65] This is why people are so disturbed when these symbols are not treated with what they regard as proper respect. Flag burning upsets many persons, for example, and the reason is that in doing this, in violating the traditional ways of treating the flag, the identity of the group is disparaged or threatened. The desecration of a national symbol is regarded as a desecration of the nation.

But traditions should not be confused with symbols. Some interpreters of religious phenomena propose to understand sacraments, doctrines, traditions, and other religious phenomena as mere symbols.[66] My concern here is not with any of these phenomena other than tradition, but I do not think traditions should be understood symbolically. Symbols are generally in the category of signs; they are connected to certain meanings. But traditions are actions that serve to connect the signs and symbols with their meanings. They are an entirely different kind of thing. Both symbols and traditions may have the effect of producing meanings, understandings, and feelings, but they do it differently. Traditions are not semantic phenomena as are signs and symbols; they are not entities selected and organized to convey meaning.[67] The flag is a symbol, whereas the action of saluting the flag on a certain occasion is a tradition. The flag functions semantically, but the tradition does not. Rather, the tradition is the action that ties us (i.e., those who salute) with the symbol (i.e., the flag) in a certain context (e.g., such as a date that commemorates a particular occasion) and as a result with each other (i.e., the nation).

The importance of symbols for social groups is supported by the fact that personal identity is closely bound up with group identity insofar as part of our identity may include our belonging to certain social groups such as nations. To be an American is very much part of Jefferson's identity. Indeed, we often feel threatened as individuals when symbols of our national identity are not treated appropriately. Belonging to a nation is related very closely to the identity of its members. Usually the persons that constitute a nation have been born in the nation or have joined it, but in either case, there is a pledge, implicit or explicit, to be part of it. To be a person is to be bound up with society.[68]

The same thing I have said about national traditions could be said about ethnic traditions, family traditions, religious traditions, and so on. This is why traditions are generally associated with a conservative attitude that seeks to preserve the past. Exchanging gifts among family members and friends at Christmas renews familial and friendship bonds. Eating turkey on Thanksgiving brings together all Americans into an act that strengthens their bonds as a nation. Observing Passover reminds Jews of who they are as a group and renews their allegiance to each other. And so on. The significance of an action for the identity of a group is a necessary condition that traditions must satisfy.

Concerning this significance, we may ask who or what determines it. Several possible answers suggest themselves: the group considered as a whole, one or more members of the group, and relations independent of the views of the group or its members. The third alternative arises, because in other cases such relations are certainly important. Consider social needs and their satisfaction. Say that a group of people is in need of medical attention. Clearly, neither the need nor what satisfies it may have anything to do with what anyone thinks about it. So, one could argue, likewise, that the significance of an action for a group is not measured, or determined, by what the group thinks, but rather by its relations to other things. Indeed, significance in general seems to work in this way.[69] Consider, for example, the significance of the conquest of the Aztec empire by Hernan Cortez. This could very well refer to the impact which the conquest had on many subsequent events, rather than the importance anyone attaches to the conquest, even if the latter may affect the former. So, the question for us is whether the significance of traditions is a matter of opinion or is independent of them.

I am sure that if our contemporaries had given sufficient thought to this—which they have not—they would fall into two camps. Realists would argue that it is a matter of relations independent of what anyone thinks, and anti-realists would claim that it is a matter merely of what people think. Both would have some good arguments in their favor. Realists could point to the fact that actions have consequences for certain persons independently of what those persons may think; and anti-realists could argue that in the realm of human relations, what people think is ultimately what affects them more clearly.

My view is that both positions are correct in their positive proposals, but incorrect in their exclusionary claims. The significance of traditions is both a matter of the consequences of the actions in question and of what people think of those actions and what they mean for the group. It is related to the consequences of actions, because these actions produce results that pull members of groups together, regardless of what they may think, and this strengthens their ties. Wine-tasting on Christmas Eve brings together our family, the celebration of Thanksgiving binds Americans, Easter draws Christians together, and Passover unites Jews. At the same time, the importance that people attach to these actions also strengthens their bonds. Thoughts about Passover unite Jews, about Easter Christians, about Thanksgiving Americans, and about wine-tasting on Christmas Eve our family. So much, then, for the requirement of significance and how it should be understood.

Let me now summarize what I have thus far suggested concerning tradition in the following formula:

X is a tradition if, and only if, it is:

(1) a voluntary and intentional action (or actions) pertaining to a group of persons that is neither arbitrary nor accidental,

(2) initiated at a certain point in history by one or more members of the group and established by the group as a whole,

(3) enacted more than once by members of the group at different and successive times, in specific contexts, with the intention of re-enacting it, and

(4) significant for the identity of the group and regarded as such by its members.

This looks very much like a definition, but if it is so, how exactly should it be taken? Definitions come in at least two main varieties: real and nominal.[70] The first aims to establish conditions of being; the second tries to establish conditions of linguistic usage. A triangle may be defined as a geometrical figure with three angles. If being a geometrical figure with three angles is taken as specifying the conditions of triangularity, we have a real definition. If, on the other hand, it is taken as making explicit the conditions under which the word 'triangle' is correctly used in English, then it is a nominal definition. Real definitions express essence whereas nominal ones make explicit linguistic usage. Philosophers are divided between those who favor linguistic definitions because they believe these are the only ones we can have, and those who favor real ones because they think these are the ones we should have. I am not going to get involved here in a discussion of the relative merits of each position, for doing so would take us far away from our main topic. I merely note that the definition of tradition I have offered is intended as a real one; I am concerned to offer an understanding of the conditions which something must satisfy in order for it to qualify as a tradition.

I should also make clear that my concern has not been focused on the psychology of tradition, that is, with the way tradition functions in, and affects, the human psyche, even if some things I have said have implications for this kind of investigation. The psychology of tradition has attracted considerable attention among certain contemporary philosophers, but I rather think that this is the province of the psychologist or the philosopher of mind.[71] In any case, this is not what has concerned me here.

Now let me turn to some objections that can be raised against the view I have proposed. Answering them will give me the opportunity to clarify further some aspects of my view that may still remain obscure.

6
Objections and Clarifications

The conception of tradition I have presented relies
heavily on some of the ordinary ways in which we
think about it. Nonetheless one might object that
this is not in fact how traditions are usually understood by philosophers, theologians, or even some
common folks, for they are very often conceived
as sets of beliefs as these were understood in chapter 4.[72] Consider, for example, that many Roman
Catholic theologians speak of the Catholic Tradition
as a set of doctrines passed down either by word of
mouth or through written texts.[73] In this sense, they
speak of an oral tradition—the doctrines or views
transmitted orally—and a written tradition—the
doctrines or views transmitted in written form. The
latter is contained in the Old and New Testaments,
and in certain authoritative texts adopted by councils
and the like. The former is contained in the words
of mouth that have not been written down or were
written down much later than the time at which
the Old and New Testaments were composed or the
councils took place.

This manner of conceiving tradition is not confined
to theology or religion; it is in fact quite common in
philosophy as well, as we saw earlier. Historians of
philosophy often speak of the Hegelian, Aristotelian,
or Kantian traditions, or they talk about the British
Empiricist tradition. By this they mean that certain
philosophers share a set of views that are fundamental

to everything else they think and which distinguishes them from those philosophers who belong to other traditions or that they consider a body of texts to be the basis of their philosophizing.[74] In the first sense, for example, Aristotelians are supposed to accept the extra-mental reality of the world and the ontological primacy of substances, among other things; Kantians are supposed to believe that the objectivity of our knowledge derives from the common mental structures that make experience possible, and so on; and similarly with the other philosophical traditions mentioned. And in the second sense, historians speak of, say, the Aristotelian tradition as a set of texts written by Aristotle and his followers that forms the basis of philosophical discussions among those who consider themselves Aristotelians.

But, we may ask: If both in theology and philosophy a common conception of tradition is as a set of doctrines or the texts used to express them, then how can my view that traditions are to be understood primarily as certain kinds of actions be considered adequate?

The answer to this objection is that conceiving traditions as sets of doctrines or texts creates the sorts of problems pointed out earlier. Moreover, it turns out that my position does preserve a place for beliefs while avoiding the difficulties with the understanding of tradition as doctrines or texts. In short, we can do better by identifying traditions with certain kinds of actions, as I have suggested. But where do beliefs fit in this scheme, for clearly I must make room for them if my position is to have any credibility?

Earlier I identified four different ways of understanding belief: three of these were propositional and the other was textual. Now let me point out a fifth understanding that is crucial for my thesis: This is the conception of belief as action. In this sense, a belief is not the propositional or textual expression of a doctrine, whether it is held or not, but rather the very action of holding the doctrine or view in question.[75] After all, 'to believe' is a verb. For X to have a belief, then, is for X to engage in an action whereby X holds that, say, there is extra-terrestrial life, that is, it is for X to believe that there is life outside the Earth.

Accordingly, when Roman Catholics talk about beliefs as constituting a tradition, for example, they can be taken to be referring to the very actions of believing rather than to certain doctrines or to their textual formulation. This view makes sense for at least two reasons: First, what counts in religious faith is the very actions of believing in which people engage and, second, ontologically it is such actions that exist—doctrines exist only insofar as someone holds them. And the same can be said about other sets of views regarded as traditions, be they legal, philosophical, or other sorts.

Consider the tradition of celebrating birthdays. This tradition, in accordance with what I have proposed, is a kind of action subject to the conditions specified in the last chapter. The knowledge of the tradition, that is, of celebrating birthdays, is stored in the memory of the members of the social group. I know and remember, for example, that I must celebrate birthdays—of my children, my wife, and even, as personally distasteful as this is, myself. In addition to having knowledge of it—to celebrate birthdays—I must also know how to do it—that is, have a set of rules that I, or others, follow in the celebration. I need to know, for example, that we need a cake and candles, that the person whose birthday is being celebrated must blow out the candles at a certain point in time, and so on. Moreover, there must also be a disposition to enact the tradition.

In addition, I must have some means of passing on both my knowledge of the tradition (that is, celebrating birthdays) and of the instructions that need to be followed to instantiate it (that is, having cake and candles), etc. The means consist of oral or written texts; the first is what I say and the second what I write. Both are means to communicate to others knowledge of the tradition and of the rules to be followed to instantiate it. My wife often has to remind me verbally of her birthday and I often write a note on my calendar about the birthdays of various members of the family in order not to forget them—actually most of the time I forget them anyway! This is why very often people think of a tradition as what is said or what is written. But this is a mistake. The tradition is the action, say, of celebrating a birthday, and what is said or written merely reflects the knowledge people have about the action and the conditions under which it is to be enacted. Of course, some traditions involve saying or writing, but this does not affect the point I am making, for it is not in virtue of the saying or writing that they are traditions.

Now that we have a proper understanding of tradition and the way belief can become part of it, I need to explain how my view avoids the difficulties raised in chapter 4 against the position which regarded tradition as belief when this is conceived as a set of propositions or texts. The two problems with the latter were that: (1) common accessibility requires tradition to become the same as texts, but this takes us back to the difficulties associated with the Hermeneutic Circle, and (2) it becomes difficult to account for the continuity of tradition.

With respect to (1), if traditions are conceived as certain kinds of actions, rather than as propositions or texts, the hermeneutic difficulty can be avoided. The first step in this direction is that, *qua* action, tradition does not function semantically, as texts and signs do, so we are already outside language when we are speaking of traditions. Actions can in certain circumstances function as texts and signs, but this is only an accidental matter, and this function is not pertinent for actions to become traditions. Recall that earlier I identified the conditions under which actions become traditions and these do not include a semantic function. The whole issue of the Hermeneutic Circle, then, does not arise. Still, difficulty (1) is not quite resolved, for we have yet to account for how communication is possible, and this requires explaining how I know that you engage in a certain action of believing—the issue of common accessibility. I deal with this difficulty in the next chapter when I explain how my view helps to break the Hermeneutic Circle, so let me set it aside for now.

With respect to (2), the problem of continuity, understanding traditions as I have proposed helps to preserve the advantages of both the Heraclitean and the Parmenidean positions while avoiding their disadvantages insofar as traditions can maintain identity in the face of change and evolution. The identity derives from several sources, five of which are particularly important: the kind of action that constitutes the tradition; the context of the action; the historical point of initiation; the intention to re-enact the tradition; and the awareness of the significance of the tradition for a group by its members. The first establishes the conditions of what we might call formal identity, separating a tradition from other traditions that involve different kinds of actions—say, eating turkey from exchanging gifts. The second establishes a specific context that separates some actions from others—eating turkey *at Thanksgiving*, rather than at any other time. The third establishes the conditions of what might be called particular identity,

distinguishing a tradition from other traditions even
in cases in which they share in the kind of action
and the context they involve—say, washing one's
hands before eating when this is done by Muslims
or by Jews. And the fourth and fifth establish the
conditions that tie instantiations of the same kind
of action in the same context by some persons to the
instantiations of those actions by other persons—say,
my celebration of Thanksgiving and your celebration
of Thanksgiving.

In the case of Thanksgiving, the tradition involves,
say, eating turkey and offering a prayer of thanks
before doing so; in the case of the Roman Catholic
Tradition it includes the actions of believing which
may take the form of saying the Creed and similar
expressions of faith; and in the case of celebrating
a birthday in the United States, it has to do with
sharing a cake, blowing out candles, singing Happy
Birthday, and so on. In all three examples, the tradition involves specific kinds of actions enacted in
specific contexts, a historical point of origin, and
an intent to re-enact the tradition on the part of
certain persons who are also aware of its significance
for the group. As long as these five conditions are
satisfied, the traditions enacted are the same. Obviously, although traditions are actions that require
more than one instantiation, multiple instantiations
at different times do not constitute an obstacle to
the preservation of their diachronic identity.[76]

These sources of identity establish also the parameters for change and evolution in particular traditions. The strength and flexibility of a particular parameter depends on the tradition in question. Some traditions are more open than others. The tradition of celebrating Christmas Eve, for example, may involve just eating a good dinner or, more specifically, eating roast pork. This means that the kinds of actions that are required for the formal identity of tradition tolerate a certain degree of flexibility, depending on the particular tradition. Likewise, the context may be similarly broad—a tradition may require that a department chair give a welcoming party for new students, but the date and parameters of the party might be quite open. The historical origin of traditions similarly fixes their particular identity while allowing for change and evolution. Finally, the intent and awareness of members of the group further supports identity without the imposition of rigid boundaries, for the intent to re-enact is open to interpretation precisely because of the group's awareness of the significance of the tradition and the elements that make it up.

Another reason why there is an opening to development and the integration of the old and the new in the understanding of tradition I have proposed, is that actions can have many relations and associations, depending on context. They elicit memories and may suggest new ways of thinking and even modes of acting compatible with them.

Actions are not bound by rigid linguistic formulas; they are performances that depend on the actors and their circumstances. There is room, then, for evolution and change in them. If the texts of the laws that regulate a nation, for example, are taken as expressing, rather than establishing, the way the citizens behave and act, that is, their ways of living, then it is the actions that are primary, and the laws considered as written formulas become secondary approximations to more fundamental realities. As such, they can be modified if indeed they are found not to adhere to the actions that they originally were thought to express, and if circumstances change, it could turn out that a certain legal formulation ceases to reflect the action which it was intended to express. Moreover, the same could be said about theological and religious texts. If these are taken to be expressions of practices, and practices are interpreted contextually, linguistic formulations which are supposed to reflect those practices might have to be changed with a change in circumstances.

In chapter 3, I raised some difficulties with the views of tradition that conceived it as content (that is, *traditum*), transmitting (*traditio*), enactment, or means. Yet, this talk is common and there seems to be something intuitively correct about it, although I have not yet seen any satisfactory explanation of it. The matter becomes clear, however, when tradition is understood as action. With respect to the identification of tradition with the content transmitted and the action of transmitting it, it becomes clear because then the content (*traditum*) and the transmission (*traditio*) become one and the same in the following way: The content is a certain kind of action (or actions) and the transmitting consists in the individual enactments of that very action (or actions), so that in both we have in fact the same kind of thing. But there is more in that this also explains why traditions are identified with enactments and the means of transmission. For, as noted, the action of transmitting and the means of transmission turn out to be the very enacted action (or actions) in question. So we have a situation in which what is transmitted—which is a way of acting—is transmitted precisely by the enactment of that way of acting, and the means used to make the transmission is precisely the action (or actions) in question.

Augustine was on the right track when he said that the way we teach is by enacting what we want to teach. To teach bird-catching one must show how to catch birds and this is done by means of the action of catching birds.[77] To put it differently, then: The passed, the passing, the enactment of the passing, and the means of passing are all one and the same, in an important sense. This explains why, as we saw earlier, traditions are often identified with the content transmitted, the action of transmitting it, the means used for the transmission, and their enactments.

But I have gone too fast. For the careful metaphysician, what I have said may not be clear enough; there may still be mysteries lurking about the corners. I need to explain in what sense exactly what is transmitted is the same as the action of transmitting it, the enacting of the tradition, and the means of transmission. But, we may ask: If all four are the same, why do we use different expressions to talk about them? Does this mean that the words are actually synonymous? It does not seem to be so, for there appears to be a sense in which what is transmitted in the tradition, the transmitting of it, its enactment, and the means of transmission are not the same.

Let me go back to a distinction proposed earlier between a universal kind of action and its individual enactments, that is, its instances. Thus, we have the universal "celebrating Thanksgiving" and the various enactments of that universal in the individual actions of Americans when they celebrate Thanksgiving, that is, for example, "this celebration of Thanksgiving," "that celebration of Thanksgiving," and so on. Metaphysically there is an important difference here, namely, the difference between a universal and its instances. Cat is one thing and this cat another. Likewise, a *traditum* is a universal kind of action and therefore something different from the *traditio*, that is, the transmitting or passing on of this universal kind of action, for the latter consists in any enacted instances of the universal. The difference, then, is not in kind, for both the *traditio* and the *traditum* consist of the same kind of action: celebrating Thanksgiving. Rather, the difference is in metaphysical status, for the *traditum* is the universal—celebrating Thanksgiving—whereas the *traditio* consists of individuals—this or that celebrating of Thanksgiving. Of course, it should be clear from this that there is no difference between the enactments and the action of transmission: traditions are transmitted by their enactments, even if they can also be transmitted in other ways.

But there is still the bit left about the means. Can we sensibly say that the means of transmission and the instance enactments of the tradition can be one and the same? Why not? This should not appear strange, for there are other cases in which the same thing does double duty. Consider the case of performatives, in which the action of apologizing is also the apology. So, why should we be concerned with the fact that an action is both an instance of a tradition and the means whereby the content of the tradition (i.e., the universal) is transmitted? What is wrong with holding that the individual actions of celebrating Thanksgiving are both instances of celebrating Thanksgiving and the means whereby the tradition of celebrating Thanksgiving is passed on? Tradition (as content) is the universal action which is enacted and which can be transmitted in (i.e., passed on) and through (i.e., by means of) its individual instantiations.

In short, understanding traditions as kinds of actions, rather than as doctrines or views, explains why tradition is variously conceived as content, transmitting, enactment, and means of transmitting. It also accounts for the common accessibility and diachronic identity of traditions and allows for the kind of flexibility required to meet the challenges of the present and the future without falling into chaos, providing continuity without ossification. Finally, this position makes possible the use of tradition for the solution of the problems identified at the beginning concerning communication, knowledge, and group identity. Let me go back to these now and show how this may be accomplished.

7
Back to Communication, Knowledge, and Group Identity

The puzzles raised at the very beginning involved three areas: communication, the transmission of knowledge, and the identity of social groups. Tradition has been suggested as a way to solve all three, but this imposes on tradition certain requirements. In the previous chapter, I proposed to satisfy these requirements with a view of tradition as action. Now I need to show how this conception helps to solve these puzzles.

A. Communication

The problem of communication arises because of our presumed inability to break the Hermeneutic Circle. Those who attempt to communicate through language are locked in texts and cannot break out of them and have access to the meanings entertained in each other's minds. As long as one tries to explain the meaning of texts through language, the analysis remains textual. But the signs of which texts are composed are polysemic, so that it is impossible to fix their meaning. It is not possible to know if the interlocutors understand the same thing, even if they use the same words.

In order to break the Hermeneutic Circle, then, one must move away from language and bring in the notion of expected behavior. But expected behavior by itself is not enough, for we need something to establish which behavior is to be expected, and this something cannot be a text, for if it is, then we cannot escape the Circle. This is sometimes and obliquely acknowledged by those who discuss tradition when they say that tradition involves transmission by means other than writing and specifically by word of mouth.[78] And others stress the oral nature of traditions. But this is not enough, for an oral transmission is still a textual transmission, and there is no qualitative difference between it and a written text. In former times, there was a sense that an oral transmission was entirely different from a written one because an oral text has a flexibility that a written one does not have. Moreover, an oral text is dependent on the author and is always contextual, whereas a written one is not.[79] But, of course, in an age when recording becomes possible, this view can no longer be maintained. An oral text is as much a text as a written one, and so to say that in the transmission of traditions no written texts play a role is not enough. We need to go beyond texts, *qua* texts, and understand that the difference in tradition and other forms of transmission is not that one consists of written and the others of oral texts, but that the transmission of traditions is non-textual.

If tradition is conceived non-textually as certain kinds of repeated actions which lack semantic import, in accordance with what I have proposed, then it can indeed be helpful in explaining how we communicate. Tradition can provide us with a map of expected behavior and this is the key to our knowledge that we communicate with each other. If I ask a waiter to bring me *tamales chiapanecos*, and he brings them to me after telling me the restaurant has them, I can be fairly certain that he has understood me, and if he brings me something else, then I should suspect that he has not.

But is this enough to answer Quine? He argued that the use of the same term is not sufficient to give us certainty that the same understanding has occurred. When I see a rabbit and the member of a tribe who does not speak English points to it and says "Gavagai," I do not know whether he is thinking about the rabbit as I do or of something quite different.

Quine is right when we are dealing with the isolated case of a word. Indeed, Quine's argument shows the need for tradition to be understood as I have proposed, but tradition does not involve just isolated words. Traditions are complex, contextual, and involve repetition. One cannot understand a language unless one understands the culture—the way of life in context of members of a society.[80] Traditions provide the underpinnings of a culture; they are the threads out of which the cultural fabric is woven. And once traditions are taken into account, the problem posed by Quine disappears. If the explorer lives with a tribe for twenty years and effectively learns their ways, then he knows what they mean when they say "Gavagai."

Still, one might respond that this does not solve the problem of communication because I still do not have access to your thoughts, only to what you say. But this is not quite right. If one holds that traditions are actions, then the door is open to accepting that, although we may not have access to some of those actions—say that I do not have access to your action of thinking that P—there are actions to which we do have access. But because the actions to which I have access and those to which I do not are part of the same framework—a way of life—the knowledge we have of some function, as keys to the knowledge of the others. The problem with the notion of tradition considered merely as a set of beliefs, when these are taken as views, is that we are locked in texts from which we cannot escape and we have no way to bridge the gap between them and acts of understanding. But when traditions are conceived as actions, texts are merely the expression of certain actions within a closely and intrinsically related framework of actions, to many of which we have access.

B. Knowledge

The second problem had to do with the transmission of knowledge. How can the scientific achievements of a generation be preserved and passed on to subsequent generations? The difficulty here is similar to the one involving the Hermeneutic Circle insofar as this knowledge is preserved in, and communicated by, linguistic formulas, and these immediately pose the problem of communication.

We find the answer, again, in tradition, provided that this is understood as universal actions of certain kinds subjected to the conditions specified in the previous chapter. The words through which knowledge of discoveries are passed on are signs used in certain ways, and these uses are part of complex sets of actions which are tied in particular contexts and ways of living and which constitute traditions. Tradition provides the connection between these words, when they are read, said, or heard, and other actions in which it is part of the tradition to engage. When I ask what 'E' stands for in the formula '$E = mc^2$', the proper action is to respond with 'energy.' As Wittgenstein would say, language is to be taken as embedded in a form of life, and this form of life is nothing but a set of closely interrelated actions of particular kinds to which we are predisposed and which are expected of us in certain contexts. This is the key to the transmission of knowledge from the past.

C. Group Identity

The third problem concerned accounting for the development and preservation of the identity of various groups, such as ethnic, national, and religious. The difficulty here varied, depending on the group. In the case of religious groups, it involved something similar to what we have encountered in the previous two cases: Even though members of a religion might accept the same linguistic formulas, we cannot be sure that the understanding of those formulas is the same for all members of the community. And if this is so, the identity of the group amounts to a verbal one. This also applies to national groups, for the laws that are supposed to unite the group are again presented in textual formulas and thus pose the problem raised by the Hermeneutic Circle.

The case with ethnic groups is different in that the difficulty here is that there do not seem to be any properties that are common to the members of the groups throughout time. How can we account, then, for the diachronic identity of the groups?

My claim is that the solution to the three problems is to be found in tradition when this is understood as certain kinds of actions that are repeated over time, for as Durkheim put it, "It is by uttering the same 'ay,' pronouncing the same word, or performing the same gesture in regard to some object that they [i.e., individual persons] become and feel themselves to be in unison."[81] A religious tradition involves certain actions in which members of the community engage. These actions may include reciting certain prayers, carrying out ceremonies, engaging in certain acts of understanding, and so on. Consider for a moment the action of consecrating the bread and the wine in the Roman Catholic mass. Certain words are uttered by the priest, certain movements of the body take place by both the priest and the congregation, certain acts of understanding occur in the priest and the audience, the priest dresses himself in a certain way, there are prescribed responses from the audience, certain music is played, and so on. In short, we have a set of actions in which everyone who is a member of the group is expected to engage in this particular situation.

Still, only some of those actions are commonly accessible, someone may wonder whether everyone in the group is actually engaging in the same kind of actions involved in understanding, say, that the bread becomes the body of Christ and the wine becomes the blood of Christ—while they perform the actions which are accessible to others. Say that Mr. X does not take this formula literally, for he thinks that the bread is still bread and the wine is still wine, and that they are only symbolically the body and blood of Christ. Yet, everything this person does is concordant with a stronger belief because he does not engage in behavior that contradicts it, such as stepping on the bread, throwing the wine on the floor, or saying he does not believe a word he is saying. Under these conditions, we must begin by noting that, as long as this contrary behavior is not present, three things are quite certain: We cannot be sure Mr. X believes something different from what other members of the congregation believe; second, those who learn by imitating him will most likely end up with beliefs similar to those of the other members of the congregation; and three, as long as the behavior of Mr. X is concordant with what is expected, how can we possibly challenge that he is not? He could be pretending, but if he is, surely we should expect that some of his behavior at some point will be different from that of other members of the community.

Liturgical acts are profoundly significant in ways that linguistic formulations are not. They constitute the enactment of beliefs, not their linguistic expression. A liturgical act, a religious rite, is much more than the words that are uttered in it, if indeed there are such words, for often there are not. This is why some theologians go so far as to argue that the liturgy provides direct contact with realities.[82] Language, by contrast, only represents for us what in the liturgy is experienced through enactment. Language is an intermediary between us and the realities which it is supposed to represent. Indeed, liturgy actually makes clear the meaning of scriptures, for it is actions that reveal the meaning of signs which are only conventionally associated with them. Signs by themselves are silent. This is one of Augustine's profound insights.

Still, some might not be satisfied, so they might ask: How can we be sure that those who enact the same kinds of actions to which we are witnesses think alike? The answer is that this issue lacks significance as long as there is no change in the actions we expect and to which we can have access. Religious traditions are neither sets of doctrines expressed in linguistic formulas nor linguistic formulas, but sets of actions, forms of acting in which certain linguistic formulas are repeated in certain circumstances as part of the fellowship within a group.

Now consider the case of nations. These are tied by laws that are supposed to govern some of the ways in which members of the nations interact. The difficulty here is that these laws exist as texts present in the memory of the citizens, or written up in libraries. So one might raise the difficulty posed by the Hermeneutic Circle in connection with them.

Again, the concept of tradition as I have proposed it is helpful, because these textual formulas are connected to expected behavior and tradition is a source of it. The written law might tell me that, if I cause the loss of an eye in someone, I also must lose an eye, and if I am the cause of someone's death, then I must also be put to death. We know members of a society understand this law when a person who caused the loss of an eye in someone else or killed someone else is himself subjected to the loss of an eye or put to death. Written laws, then, are texts tied to forms of behavior that confirm our understanding of them and unite those who accept them. To say that someone is guilty is to make a claim about a certain behavior and to expect a certain behavior on the part of various members of society.

The answer to Quine, then, is that his argument about 'Gavagai' makes sense only when its utterance is taken in isolation and divorced from a way of life. This case poses a problem because it is isolated from the way of life of which it is a part, for it is only within such a way of life that "we ask questions, carry out investigations, and make judgments."[83] To try to figure out what 'Gavagai' means outside the way of life in which it is embedded is impossible. I have to learn the way of life before I can understand the word. When I do, I am able to see that perhaps 'Gavagai' is actually 'Ga vaga i' and that it means "running furry thing," because it is also applied to cats when they are running. Or I might discover that it means "animal who nurses," and thus that it would be similar to what we call mammals. Or still, it might turn out that it means "substance of a rabbit kind," because it is applied only to things that in English are called substances. And so on. Only someone acquainted with two ways of living can attempt to translate from one language into another, for learning a foreign language involves a perspective on one's previous worldview, and it is the way we live that makes this possible.[84] Learning a language is nothing but learning a way of living,[85] for language, plucked from its context, as postmodernists frequently and rightly proclaim, is highly ambiguous.[86]

Nonetheless, someone might come back to the recurrent point that, even if we engage in the same outwardly perspicuous practices, we still do not know what each of us thinks. But this is to miss the point, for it makes no sense to ask what each of us thinks from, as it were, the outside; questions make sense only in the context of a way of life. A question posed outside its life context creates an artificial situation and violates the very conditions of communication and meaning. To ask it is to make a category mistake—as Ryle would put it—or a type mistake—as Carnap would say.[87] If I ask an English speaker what 'eating' means, the person would either give me a linguistic description of it, point to someone eating, or engage in the action of eating to illustrate what it means. And if I were to say that this is all very well, but I still do not know what she thinks when she thinks about eating, and that I need further proof of what it is, the person would throw up her hands in desperation and say that I was either an idiot, a foreigner, or nuts. And with reason, because my behavior does not accord with the expectations of the person under the circumstances and makes no sense. To know the meaning of 'eating' is precisely to be able to use the word appropriately in a community of English speakers. This is the force of the much discussed Wittgensteinian view that meaning is use.

In short, questions about what people mean and understand make sense only within a linguistic framework that reflects a way of life and in the context of which such words are used. To take words out of that context creates an artificial situation which leads to unresolvable paradoxes, such as the one raised by Quine. The reason is obvious: Outside the way of life within which these words are used effectively, there are no criteria or rules that can be applied to them. The way of life, then, establishes the boundaries of human action and thus of speech.

Finally, with respect to ethnic groups, we may ask: How can tradition help us to account for their diachronic identity, when the groups do not appear to share common features throughout their existence? The answer is that these groups are tied by certain historical relations that, although they may change over time, are continuous with each other and are mostly cashed out in terms of actions that tie the members of the groups with each other while separating them from other groups. Traditions, then, as kinds of repeated actions, are part of the social glue that binds the members of these groups. Eating turkey on Thanksgiving, celebrating the feast of the Epiphany by giving gifts to children, and so on, are all patterns of behavior that can be considered traditions and help keep ethnic groups together. At the same time, the flexibility that traditions provide explains how the particular features that might characterize an ethnic group at some point might change over time.

D. Three Significant Consequences

Contrary to what some might expect, none of this means that linguistic formulas are to be regarded as irrelevant or useless, whether they express laws, creeds, doctrines, definitions, and so on. Of course, they are important! Religious groups cannot do away with their doctrinal formulations and creeds;

nations cannot forfeit their written laws; and we need linguistic statements from the past to get at past knowledge. But these linguistic formulas have to be taken as residues of behavior, that is, of actions that fit into a way of life, rather than as isolated phenomena, independent of that way of life. Only in context can they help us understand each other and indentify with each other.

This view has at least three important consequences that should not be overlooked. There are others as well for whose exploration I have no space here. First, if traditions are not ultimately to be taken as propositions or their linguistic expressions, then they should be judged not by the criterion of consistency, but by that of compatibility. And compatibility, in contrast with consistency, is more flexible—its boundaries are less sharp and it is open to compromise. Reality is not an either/or, but rather a more/less, affair.

Practices and actions are not contradictory or non-contradictory, for the Law of Non-Contradiction applies only to propositions and the sentences that express them, where clear demarcations can be set. Practices and actions should rather be judged as compatible or incompatible with each other. It may be incompatible for me to type and handwrite at the same time, but the action of typing does not contradict the action of handwriting. In the laws of a nation what counts is that the actions in which one engages are compatible with the practices the written laws aim to express. Likewise, in a religious tradition,

what is most important is the compatibility of the
practices in which members engage. Membership in
the group depends on the compatibility of practices
with those in which the religious group engages. As
long as I do what other members of the group do and
nothing that is incompatible with it, I am a member
of the group. Ultimately, what matters is what I do,
which explains why some theologians emphasize
harmony and fellowship, rather than consistency,
when they speak of religious communities.

The realization that traditions are not linguistic in
turn leads to the two other consequences to which I
referred that are especially important in the case of
nations and religions. One is the need for humility;
we should become more humble when it comes to
the claims that we make about others. If the unity
of a nation has to do with practices, then as long
as those are carried out, how can we question the
patriotism of others merely on the basis of words?
And something similar applies to religion: If religion
has to do primarily with practices, then how can I
question the orthodoxy of persons engaged in the
common practices of the religious group even if some
of what they say differs from what is deemed to be
the standard formulations of an orthodox view?

The other consequence is the need for tolerance.
The tendency in groups, whether ethnic, religious,
or national, is to become intolerant, to draw sharp
lines between the pure and the impure, the orthodox and the unorthodox, and the good citizens and

those who are not, on the basis of rigid linguistic formulas. Any departure from what are regarded as fundamental (thus the term 'fundamentalists') sets of formulas, is taken as anathema, even if the accused continue to live lives concordant with the practices of the group. But does this make sense?

Ethnicity, religion, and nationality are not primarily matters of linguistic formulations, but of practices. They do not have to do primarily with language, but rather with ways of living. Does this mean that I am advocating a disregard for the formulation of doctrines and founding religions on a kind of mystical mush? To repeat what I have already stated: No. Clearly, linguistic formulas are important, but we must keep in mind that they are expressions of a way of life shared by members of a group.[88] Some religions have been obsessed with heresy, and in their zeal to root it out, they have often forgotten that religion is fundamentally a way of life. The preoccupation with disagreement and the purity of the faith has pushed churches to extreme versions of what I like to call *verbalism*, the view that religion is merely a matter of linguistic formulas or of adhering to linguistic formulas. But if we examine the canonical scriptures of most major religions, the lives of their founders had little to do with this zeal.

Ask yourselves, for example, how many times Christ grilled the Apostles on the exact linguistic formulas to which they should adhere? Surely there are texts in which he did express concern for the way the Apostles expressed themselves, but mostly he seems to have taught by example, and when explicitly instructing, with parables, which again show how we should live, rather than establish a linguistic code to which we need to adhere. It is deeds that count, not words. Whence comes the wisdom of the popular saying: "Sticks and stones may break my bones, but names will never hurt me." Words are merely one of the means we use to communicate about deeds. Words should matter only when they matter—to put it trivially. But when do they matter? When they affect our actions. A heretic is not someone who considers, expresses, or even argues for formulations that seem to be new or different from those generally accepted by a religious group. Heretics are people who sever themselves from the life of the community, members who cease to break bread with the rest, and whose actions reveal that they have rejected fellowship.

To paraphrase Wittgenstein: Faith is not a matter of language but of a form of life.[89] It has to do fundamentally with living in a certain way, for it is this way of life that confers religious meaning and binds the community.[90] To say that one believes in God is not primarily the utterance of a linguistic formula; rather, it is a profession of faith. And 'faith' in this context means most of all that one is committed to a certain course of action or that one has dispositions to act in certain ways in particular circumstances, even if the course of action in question is precisely to hold a certain proposition to be true. As some theologians point out, the hermeneutic of symbols resembles a liturgical act, that is, a sacred action that, as such, does not require a philosopher, but a priest.[91] The relation between the members of a community of believers is not one of speakers; it is not a matter of conversation, but of communion, that is, of union in a common set of practices that tie them together.[92]

Old Wine in New Skins

In conclusion, let me express the understanding of tradition I have proposed by saying that tradition is in some fundamental ways like old wine in new skins. The reference is to the well-known verses of Matthew 9:17, Mark 2:22, and Luke 5:37, in which we are told that the knowledgeable person does not put new wine in old skins, for doing so only serves to make the skins burst.

How does this metaphor enlighten us about our issue? Because it illustrates that the past can continue in the present and the present can integrate the past. Disregarding the new context in the understanding of the old is like putting new wine in old skins: The old skins burst and the wine is spilled and lost. But taking into account the new context in the consideration of the old is like putting old wine in new skins: The wine is modified while remaining the same in significant ways. Wine is easily affected by its surroundings, and when put in new skins, these have an effect on its taste and aroma. And the new skins are also changed, for they absorb some of the wine and become suffused with its character. But there is nothing artificial or forced about this process in that it is in the nature of a wine skin to have wine inside it, and it is in the nature of wine to be in a wine skin. This is a close association in which the particular nature of the relata affect each other in fundamental ways while maintaining their respective identities.

I understand this to mean that the present can incorporate the past and the future can incorporate both the past and the present without implying radical changes in either the present or the past. The idea so often repeated, that tradition can be fixed in writing, contradicts everything that those who believe in tradition say about it; writing can fix nothing insofar as it depends on interpretation and interpretation is a function of culture, that is, of the way interpreters live.[93] This is the force of the scriptural formula and the core of tradition.

Understanding this truth, however, is by no means easy. Accordingly, in this lecture I began by pointing out certain puzzles for the solution to which the notion of tradition is useful. These concerned communication, the transmission of knowledge, and the identity of social groups. This led me in turn to the consideration of several conceptions of tradition, all of which were found to be wanting. I argued against the view that tradition is history, a habit, texts, language, or mere custom. Moreover, we found that ultimately the *prima facie* viable views of tradition reduced to two fundamental understandings of it: as belief or as action. Of these, the first proved to be unacceptable, so I next presented a conception of tradition in terms of certain kinds of voluntary and intentional actions that are repeated by members of social groups and are significant for their identity. Finally, I claimed that this view of tradition helps us to solve the puzzles posed by communication, the transmission of knowledge, and group identity, and therefore, that tradition plays a key role in our understanding of each other, in the preservation of knowledge, and in our social organization.

Notes

1. Cf. Hans-Georg Gadamer, *Truth and Method*, 2nd rev. ed, trans. rev. by Joel Weinsheimer and Donald G. Marshall (New York: Continuum, 2002), p. 280. J. R. Geiselmann claims an essential link between religion and tradition in *The Meaning of Tradition* (New York: Herder and Herder, 1966), p. 81.

2. Walter Benjamin, "Über einige Motive bei Baudelaire," in *Illuminationen* (Frankfurt a. M.: Suhrkamp, 1980), p. 186.

3. A. Giddens, *The Consequences of Modernity* (Cambridge: Polity Press, 1990), p. 105. For some of the ways in which globalization affects us, see M. Featherstone, ed., *Global Culture: Nationalism, Globalization and Modernity* (London: Sage, 1990).

4. Edward Shils, *Tradition* (London: Farber and Farber, 1981).

5. The closest we get to an in-depth investigation of tradition in philosophy are Gadamer's *Truth and Method* and Alasdair MacIntyre, *Whose Justice? Which Rationality?* (Notre Dame, IN: University of Notre Dame Press, 1988). But in neither of these is tradition the central topic of discussion, or systematically treated.

6. Shils, *Tradition*, pp. 7-10.

7. Monserrat Guibernau, *Nationalisms: The Nation-State and Nationalism in the Twentieth Century* (Cambridge: Polity Press, 1996), pp. 133 and 142; Yves Congar, *The Meaning of Tradition*, trans. A. N. Woodrow (New York: Hawthorn Books, 1964), pp. 7-8, 144 -145, *et passim*.

8. Cf. George Allan, *The Importances of the Past: A Meditation on the Authority of Tradition* (Albany, NY: State University of New York Press, 1986), p. 199.

9. Cf. MacIntyre, *Whose Justice? Which Rationality?*, p. 7; and Basil Mitchell, "Tradition," in Philip L. Quinn

and Charles Taliaferro, eds., *A Companion to Philosophy of Religion* (Oxford: Blackwell Publishers, 1997), p. 592.

[10] Among the authors who have provided the foundation for this point of view are Michel Foucault and Jacques Derrida.

[11] Heinrich Schmid, *The Doctrinal Theology of the Evangelical Lutheran Church*, 3rd rev. ed., trans. by Charles A. Hay and Henry E. Jacobs (Minneapolis, MN: Augsbury, 1961), pp. 58 ff.

[12] See MacIntyre, *Whose Justice? Which Rationality?*, ch. 19; and Jorge J. E. Gracia, *A Theory of Textuality: The Logic and Epistemology* (Albany, NY: State University of New York Press, 1995), pp. 207-213.

[13] Angelika Rauch, *The Hieroglyph of Tradition: Freud, Benjamin, Gadamer, Novalis, Kant* (Cranbury, NJ: Associated University Presses, 2000), ch. 11.

[14] Guibernau, *Nationalisms*, p. 133.

[15] There are many different formulations and interpretations of the Hermeneutic Circle. For reasons of parsimony, I dispense with discussion of these here and simply present my own view. For some other views, see: Stanley Rosen, "The Limits of Interpretation," in Anthony Cascardi, ed., *Literature and the Question of Philosophy* (Baltimore, MD: Johns Hopkins University Press, 1987), p. 224; John M. Connolly and Thomas Keutner, trans. and eds., *Hermeneutics versus Science? Three German Views* (Notre Dame, IN: University of Notre Dame Press, 1988), p. 7; Wolfgang Stegmüller, "Walther von der Vogelweide's Lyric of Dream-Love and Quasar 3C273: Reflections on the So-Called 'Circle of Understanding' and on the So-Called 'Theory-Ladenness of Observation,'" trans. John Connolly and Thomas Keutner, in *Hermeneutics versus Science?*, pp. 104 and 110 ff; Gadamer, "On the Circle of Understanding," trans. John Connolly and Thomas Keutner,

in *Hermeneutics versus Science?*, pp. 68 ff; Günther Buck, "The Structure of Hermeneutic Experience and the Problem of Tradition," *New Literary History* 10 (1978): 32; and Jacques Derrida, "Structure, Sign, and Play in the Discourse of the Human Sciences," in R. Macksay and E. Donato, eds., *The Structuralist Controversy: The Languages of Criticism and the Sciences of Man* (Baltimore, MD: Johns Hopkins University Press, 1970), p. 250. For some particular formulations in the context of revelation and theology, see Gracia, "Revelation under Fire: Meeting the Challenges of the Hermeneutic Circle," *American Catholic Philosophical Quarterly* (2003), forthcoming.

[16] Augustine, *De Magistro*, ch. 10, § 33, ed. by Victorino Capanaga, *et al.*, in *Obras de San Agustín* (Madrid: Biblioteca de Autores Cristianos, 1971), p. 623. The problem goes back to Plato; see, in particular, the *Meno*.

[17] Gracia, *A Theory of Textuality*, p. 193.

[18] I defend this view in Gracia, *A Theory of Textuality*, p. 4.

[19] W. V. O. Quine, "On What There Is," in *From a Logical Point of View* (Cambridge, MA: Harvard University Press, 1953), p. 17. See also "Two Dogmas of Empiricism," in the same volume.

[20] I have dealt with this issue in some detail in Gracia, *Hispanic/Latino Identity,* particularly chapter 3, where I also refer to the pertinent literature.

[21] As John McCole finds regarding Walter Benjamin in *Walter Benjamin and the Antinomies of Tradition* (Ithaca, NY: Cornell University Press, 1993), pp. 10 and 295. Yves Congar notes that tradition involves both continuity and progress, in *The Meaning of Tradition*, pp. 145-146.

[22] T. S. Eliot, "Tradition and the Individual Talent," in *Selected Essays 1917-1932* (London: Faber and Faber, 1932), pp. 17 and 16. A similar point is echoed by

Harold Bloom, *A Map of Misreading* (New York: Oxford University Press, 1975), p. 19.

[23] MacIntyre, *Whose Justice? Which Rationality?*, p. 387.

[24] Congar, *The Meaning of Tradition,* p. 105.

[25] For the discussion of identity in section A, I largely rely on Gracia, *Hispanic/Latino Identity,* ch. 2.

[26] An alternative formulation would be: X is identical with Y, if and only if there is no F of X that Y does not have, and vice versa. The problem with this formulation is that for it to work, an entity would have to include something other than its features, and this certainly is not a universally accepted view. For this reason, I adopt the more encompassing formulation given in the body of the text.

[27] The view I am proposing should not be confused with that proposed by Peter Geach. There is no general agreement on the best way to understand similarity and identity. For a different understanding of them from the one provided here, see Andrew Brennan, *Conditions of Identity: A Study of Identity and Survival* (Oxford: Clarendon Press, 1988), p. 6.

[28] I discuss this and other related issues in Gracia, *Introduction to the Problem of Individuation in the Early Middle Ages,* 2nd rev. edition (Munich: Philosophia Verlag, 1988), p. 26.

[29] Sociologists acknowledge this point in the context of social groups in particular. T. H. Eriksen, "Ethnicity, Race, and Nation," in M. Guibernau and J. Rex, eds., *The Ethnicity Reader: Nationalism, Multiculturalism and Migration* (Cambridge: Polity Press, 1997), p. 37.

[30] These are frequently conflated; indeed, identity in general is often taken to include diachronicity. See, for example, Guibernau, *Nationalisms,* p. 73.

[31] Roderick Chisholm, "Identity Through Time," in H. E. Kiefer and M. K. Munitz, eds., *Language, Belief, and Metaphysics* (Albany, NY: State University of New York

Press, 1970), pp. 163-182. Diachronic identity should not be confused with duration. Duration requires that something be identical at two or more different times (diachronic identity) and that it be so throughout the time elapsed between those times. The conditions of duration involve more than the conditions of diachronic identity. See Gracia, *Texts: Ontological Status, Identity, Author, Audience* (Albany, NY: State University of New York Press, 1996), pp. 69-79. Interrupted duration involves diachronic identity only at some times.

32 R. Baumeister, *Identity: Cultural Change and Struggle for Self* (Oxford: Oxford University Press, 1986), pp. 18-19.

33 This distinction is frequently, but not universally, ignored in the literature. See, for example, J. Butler, "Conversational Break: A Reply to Robert Gooding-Williams," in Robert Bernasconi, ed., *Race* (Oxford: Blackwell, 2001), p. 263.

34 Gorgias, *On Nature*, in John Mansley Robinson, *An Introduction to Early Greek Philosophy*, Appendix B (New York: Houghton Mifflin, 1968), p. 295.

35 Gadamer, *Truth and Method*, p. 357; Martin Heidegger, *The Concept of Time*, trans. William McNeill (Oxford: Blackwell, 1992), p. 19.

36 For literature on this issue, see: Benedict Anderson, *Imagined Communities* (London: Verso Editions/NLB, 1983); Bob Carter, *Realism and Racism* (London: Routledge, 2000); and Guibernau and Rex, *Ethnicity Reader*. One source of this view is Michel Foucault, *The Order of Things: An Archaeology of the Human Sciences* (New York: Vintage Books, 1973), particularly the Preface.

37 The bearer of tradition is often referred to as "its subject" in the literature. Congar, *The Meaning of Tradition*, chapter 2.

38 See, for example, the different ways in which Congar refers to the content of tradition in *The Meaning of*

Tradition, pp. 118 ff., *et passim.* See also Shils, *Tradition,* pp. 12-13, 16-17, and 31.

39 For P. F. Strawson's view, see *Individuals: An Essay in Descriptive Metaphysics* (London: Methuen and Co., 1959), Preface; for my position on this issue, see Gracia, *Individuality: An Essay on the Foundations of Metaphysics* (Albany, NY: State University of New York Press, 1988), pp. xiv-xvi, and *Metaphysics and Its Task: The Search for the Categorial Foundation of Knowledge* (Albany, NY: State University of New York Press, 1999), pp. 94-98 and 142-143.

40 *The Compact Edition of the Oxford English Dictionary* (Oxford: Oxford University Press, 1971).

41 Paul Evdokimov, *L'Orthodoxie* (Neuchâtel: Delachaux et Niestlé, 1959), p. 195

42 Shils, *Tradition*, p. 12.

43 Shils refers to many of these and others in *Tradition,* pp. 12-13; and theologians also cite many examples. See Congar, *The Meaning of Tradition,* pp. 17-18.

44 In *Whose Justice? Which Rationality?*, MacIntyre speaks of traditions as "bodies of systematic beliefs," as "ways of understanding. . .the world," (p. 352) and as "core[s] of shared beliefs" (p. 356). He also speaks of the linguistic embodiment of traditions (p. 371), the beliefs that characterize traditions (p. 383), and of beliefs that are shared by those who adhere to traditions (p. 388). See also Mitchell, "Tradition," p. 591.

45 Gadamer identifies tradition with language in *Truth and Method*, pp. 358, 389, and 463, and texts are nothing but language in use.

46 This is a position *à la* Hume, and it is perhaps the one Allan has in mind in *The Importances of the Past*, p. 240.

47 See Sanford Budick, *The Western Theory of Tradition: Terms and Paradigms of the Cultural Sublime* (New Haven, CT: Yale University Press, 2000).

48 Basil Mitchell, *Faith and Criticism* (Oxford: Clarendon Press, 1994), p. 3; see also p. 109.

49 But perhaps even this is not quite right. See my extended discussion of the identity conditions of texts in Gracia, *Texts*, ch. 2.

50 I have defended this view in Gracia, *Individuality*, chapter 1.

51 See chapter 2 of ibid.

52 Ibid.

53 See, for example: D. M. Armstrong, *A Materialist Theory of Mind* (London: Routledge & Kegan Paul, 1968); Elizabeth Prior, *Dispositions* (Aberdeen: Aberdeen University Press, 1985); and Gilbert Ryle, *The Concept of Mind* (London: Hutchinson, 1949).

54 Not everyone agrees with this realist view. For a non-realist position, see Ryle, *The Concept of Mind*. For realist views, see: N. Goodman, *Facts, Fiction, and Forecast*, 2nd ed. (Indianapolis, IN: Bobbs-Merrill, 1965), and Armstrong, *A Materialist Theory of Mind*.

55 Note that whether one adopts a physicalist or a non-physicalist conception of mind is irrelevant for the claims I have made and the issues I am addressing.

56 Aquinas, *Summa theologiae* I-II, 53, 2 and 3.

57 Foucault, *The Order of Things*, particularly the Preface; and Ian Hacking, "Making Up People," in Thomas C. Heller *et al.*, eds., *Reconstructing Individualism: Autonomy, Individuality and the Self in Western Thought* (Stanford, CA: Stanford University Press, 1986), pp. 222-236.

58 Guibernau, *Nationalisms*, p. 133.

59 I have discussed this issue in detail in Gracia, *Hispanic/Latino Identity*, chapters 1, 3, and 5.

60 For ethnic conceptions of race, see: Linda Alcoff, "Is Latino/a Identity a Racial Identity?" in Jorge J. E. Gracia and Pablo De Greiff, eds., *Hispanics/Latinos in the United States: Ethnicity, Race, and Rights* (New York:

Routledge, 2000), pp. 23-44; and David T. Goldberg, *Racist Culture: Philosophy and the Politics of Meaning* (Oxford: Blackwell, 1993).

[61] This is the traditional view of race found, for example, in J. F. Blumenbach, "On the Natural Variety of Mankind," trans. Thomas Bendyshe, in Robert Bernasconi and Tommy Lott, eds., *The Idea of Race* (Bloomington, IN: Hackett, 2000), pp. 27-37. I discuss this and other views of race in some detail in chapter 4 of Gracia, *Surviving Race, Ethnicity, and Nationality: A Foundational Analysis for the Twenty-First Century* (forthcoming).

[62] Customs can also be individual, a fact that distinguishes traditions from customs when the latter are considered in general, but individual customs do not pose a challenge to my claim that traditions are social.

[63] In *The Importances of the Past,* Allan cashes out this significance in terms of the importance that traditions have for connecting us to structures of meaning from the past and for sustaining that connection. This suggestion deserves the kind of discussion that I cannot give it here because of limitations of space.

[64] I defend this conception of a nation in chapter 5 of Gracia, *Surviving Race, Ethnicity, and Nationality.*

[65] Guibernau, *Nationalisms,* p. 133.

[66] John Henry (Cardinal) Newman argues against this position in *Letters and Correspondence of John Henry Newman During His Life in the English Church,* ed. Anne Mozley (London: Longmans, Green, and Co., 1891), vol 2, pp. 155-156.

[67] For a discussion of the nature of signs, see Gracia, *A Theory of Textuality*, pp. 7-14.

[68] Aristotle acknowledges the social nature of humans in *Nicomachean Ethics* 1097b11, 1162a17, and in *Politics* 1253a7, but he also suggests in the first work that humans are to be identified with their intellect (*nous*) at 1178a7-8, without providing the means to synthesize

the two accounts. For an account that attempts to do so, see Part II, pp. 370-595 of Max Scheler's *Formalism in Ethics and Non-Formal Ethics of Values*, trans. Manfred S. Frings and Roger L. Funk (Evanston, IL: Northwestern University Press, 1973). For a discussion of this issue, see Jonathan J. Sanford's *Aristotle, Scheler, MacIntyre: The Metaphysical Foundations of Ethics*, doctoral dissertation (State University of New York at Buffalo, 2001), and Gracia, *Surviving Race, Ethnicity, and Nationality*, ch. 7.

[69] See E. D. Hirsch, Jr., "Three Dimensions of Hermeneutics," *New Literary History* 3 (1972), 249-250; Gracia, *A Theory of Textuality*, pp. 18-19; and William Irwin, *Intentionalist Interpretations: A Philosophical Explanation and Defense* (Westport, CT: Greenwood Press, 1999), pp. 46-50.

[70] For the different kinds of definitions, see Richard Robinson, *Definitions* (Oxford: Clarendon Press, 1954).

[71] This seems to be Rauch's main concern in *The Hieroglyph of Tradition*, for example.

[72] See, for example, Mark Bevir, *The Logic of the History of Ideas* (Cambridge: Cambridge University Press, 2000), p. 313; also Günther Biemer, *Newman on Tradition,* trans. and ed. Kevin Smyth (New York: Herder and Herder, 1967), pp. 140-142.

[73] Congar, *The Meaning of Tradition*, p. 98 *et passim*.

[74] MacIntyre, *Whose Justice? Which Rationality?*, pp. 352, 374, 388, *et passim*.

[75] Aquinas, *Summa theologiae* II-II, 2, 1.

[76] Their multiple instantiation is sometimes raised as a difficulty for their diachronic identity, but see what Gadamer has to say about festivities, in *Truth and Method*, p. 123.

[77] Augustine, *De Magistro*, ch. 10, § 32, p. 622.

[78] Congar, *The Meaning of Tradition,* pp. 18 and 19.

[79] See Plato, *Phaedrus* 275, and Paul Ricoeur, *Hermeneutics and the Human Sciences,* ed. J. Thompson (Cambridge: Cambridge University Press, 1989), p. 108.

[80] MacIntyre, *Whose Justice? Which Rationality?,* p. 377.

[81] Émile Durkheim, *The Elementary Forms of the Religious Life,* trans. J. W. Swain (London: George Allen, 1982), p. 230. See also Gadamer, *Truth and Method,* p. 571.

[82] Congar, *The Meaning of Tradition,* p. 129.

[83] Norman Malcolm, *Reason and Religion,* ed. Stuart Brown (Ithaca, NY: Cornell University Press, 1977), p. 146.

[84] Cf. Gadamer, *Truth and Method,* p. 441.

[85] MacIntyre, *Whose Justice? Which Rationality?,* p. 382.

[86] Roland Barthes, *Critique et Vérité* (Paris: Éditions du Seuil, 1966), pp. 49-56.

[87] Ryle, *The Concept of Mind,* and Rudolph Carnap, "The Elimination of Metaphysics through Logical Analysis of Language," trans. Arthur Pap, in A. J. Ayer, ed., *Logical Positivism* (Glencoe, IL: Free Press, 1959), pp. 60-81.

[88] Geiselmann points out a significant fact in *The Meaning of Tradition,* p. 88: "Religious formulas are handed down in the performance of ritual."

[89] Wittgenstein, *Philosophical Investigations* § 241, trans. G. E. M. Anscombe (New York: Macmillan, 1965), p. 88e.

[90] Evdokimov, *L'Orthodoxie,* p. 195.

[91] Cf. R. Panikkar, *Myth, Faith and Hermeneutics* (New York: Paulist Press, 1979), p. 135.

[92] Ibid., pp. 245-246.

[93] O. Cullmann, *La Tradition: Problème exégétique, historique et théologique* (Neuchatel: Delachaux et Niestlè, 1953), p. 44. See also a less strong formulation of this view in Congar, *The Meaning of Tradition,* p. 95. I have defended cultural function in the interpretation of texts in Gracia, *A Theory of Textuality,* ch. 5.

THE AQUINAS LECTURES
Published by the Marquette University Press
Milwaukee WI 53201-1881 USA
All volumes available as ebooks. See web page:
http://www.mu.edu/mupress/

1. *St. Thomas and the Life of Learning.* John F. McCormick, S.J. (1937) ISBN 0-87462-101-1
2. *St. Thomas and the Gentiles.* Mortimer J. Adler (1938) ISBN 0-87462-102-X
3. *St. Thomas and the Greeks.* Anton C. Pegis (1939) ISBN 0-87462-103-8
4. *The Nature and Functions of Authority.* Yves Simon (1940) ISBN 0-87462-104-6
5. *St. Thomas and Analogy.* Gerald B. Phelan (1941) ISBN 0-87462-105-4
6. *St. Thomas and the Problem of Evil.* Jacques Maritain (1942) ISBN 0-87462-106-2
7. *Humanism and Theology.* Werner Jaeger (1943) ISBN 0-87462-107-0
8. *The Nature and Origins of Scientism.* John Wellmuth (1944) ISBN 0-87462-108-9
9. *Cicero in the Courtroom of St. Thomas Aquinas.* E.K. Rand (1945) ISBN 0-87462-109-7
10. *St. Thomas and Epistemology.* Louis-Marie Regis, O.P. (1946) ISBN 0-87462-110-0
11. *St. Thomas and the Greek Moralists.* Vernon J.Bourke (1947) ISBN 0-87462-111-9
12. *History of Philosophy and Philosophical Education.* Étienne Gilson (1947) ISBN 0-87462-112-7
13. *The Natural Desire for God.* William R.O'Connor (1948) ISBN 0-87462-113-5
14. *St. Thomas and the World State.* Robert M. Hutchins (1949) ISBN 0-87462-114-3

15. *Method in Metaphysics.* Robert J. Henle, S.J. (1950) ISBN 0-87462-115-1

16. *Wisdom and Love in St. Thomas Aquinas.* Étienne Gilson (1951) ISBN 0-87462-116-X

17. *The Good in Existential Metaphysics.* Elizabeth G. Salmon (1952) ISBN 0-87462-117-8

18. *St. Thomas and the Object of Geometry.* Vincent E. Smith (1953) ISBN 0-87462-118-6

19. *Realism And Nominalism Revisted.* Henry Veatch (1954) ISBN 0-87462-119-4

20. *Imprudence in St. Thomas Aquinas.* Charles J. O'Neil (1955) ISBN 0-87462-120-8

21. *The Truth That Frees.* Gerard Smith, S.J. (1956) ISBN 0-87462-121-6

22. *St. Thomas and the Future of Metaphysics.* Joseph Owens, C.Ss.R. (1957) ISBN 0-87462-122-4

23. *Thomas and the Physics of 1958: A Confrontation.* Henry Margenau (1958) ISBN 0-87462-123-2

24. *Metaphysics and Ideology.* Wm. Oliver Martin (1959) ISBN 0-87462-124-0

25. *Language, Truth and Poetry.* Victor M. Hamm (1960) ISBN 0-87462-125-9

26. *Metaphysics and Historicity.* Emil L. Fackenheim (1961) ISBN 0-87462-126-7

27. *The Lure of Wisdom.* James D. Collins (1962) ISBN 0-87462-127-5

28. *Religion and Art.* Paul Weiss (1963) ISBN 0-87462-128-3

29. *St. Thomas and Philosophy.* Anton C. Pegis (1964) ISBN 0-87462-129-1

30. *The University in Process.* John O. Riedl (1965) ISBN 0-87462-130-5

31. *The Pragmatic Meaning of God.* Robert O. Johann (1966) ISBN 0-87462-131-3

32. *Religion and Empiricism.* John E. Smith (1967)
   ISBN 0-87462-132-1
33. *The Subject.* Bernard Lonergan, S.J. (1968)
   ISBN 0-87462-133-X
34. *Beyond Trinity.* Bernard J. Cooke (1969)
   ISBN 0-87462-134-8
35. *Ideas and Concepts.* Julius R. Weinberg (1970)
   ISBN 0-87462-135-6
36. *Reason and Faith Revisited.* Francis H. Parker (1971)
   ISBN 0-87462-136-4
37. *Psyche and Cerebrum.* John N. Findlay (1972)
   ISBN 0-87462-137-2
38. *The Problem of the Criterion.* Roderick M. Chisholm
   (1973) ISBN 0-87462-138-0
39. *Man as Infinite Spirit.* James H. Robb (1974)
   ISBN 0-87462-139-9
40. *Aquinas to Whitehead: Seven Centuries of Metaphysics
   of Religion.* Charles Hartshorne (1976)
   ISBN 0-87462-141-0
41. *The Problem of Evil.* Errol E. Harris (1977)
   ISBN 0-87462-142-9
42. *The Catholic University and the Faith.* Francis C. Wade,
   S.J. (1978) ISBN 0-87462-143-7
43. *St. Thomas and Historicity.* Armand J. Maurer, C.S.B.
   (1979) ISBN 0-87462-144-5
44. *Does God Have a Nature?* Alvin Plantinga (1980)
   ISBN 0-87462-145-3
45. *Rhyme and Reason: St. Thomas and Modes of Discourse.*
   Ralph Mcinerny (1981) ISBN 0-87462-148-8
46. *The Gift: Creation.* Kenneth L. Schmitz (1982)
   ISBN 0-87462-149-6
47. *How Philosophy Begins.* Beatrice H. Zedler (1983)
   ISBN 0-87462-151-8
48. *The Reality of the Historical Past.* Paul Ricoeur (1984)
   ISBN 0-87462-152-6

49. *Human Ends and Human Actions: An Exploration in St. Thomas' Treatment.* Alan Donagan (1985) ISBN 0-87462-153-4

50. *Imagination and Metaphysics in St. Augustine.* Robert O'Connell, S.J. (1986) ISBN 0-87462-227-1

51. *Expectations of Immortality in Late Antiquity.* Hilary A Armstrong (1987) ISBN 0-87462-154-2

52. *The Self.* Anthony Kenny (1988) ISBN 0-87462-155-0

53. *The Nature of Philosophical Inquiry.* Quentin Lauer, S.J. (1989) ISBN 0-87562-156-9

54. *First Principles, Final Ends and Contemporary Philosophical Issues.* Alasdair MacIntyre (1990) ISBN 0-87462-157-7

55. *Descartes among the Scholastics.* Marjorie Greene (1991) ISBN 0-87462-158-5

56. *The Inference That Makes Science.* Ernan McMullin (1992) ISBN 0-87462-159-3

57. *Person and Being.* W. Norris Clarke, S.J. (1993) ISBN 0-87462-160-7

58. *Metaphysics and Culture.* Louis Dupré (1994) ISBN 0-87462-161-5

59. *Mediæval Reactions to the Encounters between Faith and Reason.* John F. Wippel (1995) ISBN 0-87462-162-3

60. *Paradoxes of Time in Saint Augustine.* Roland J. Teske, S.J. (1996) ISBN 0-87462-163-1

61. *Simplicity As Evidence of Truth.* Richard Swinburne (1997) ISBN 0-87462-164-X

62. *Science, Religion and Authority: Lessons from the Galileo Affair.* Richard J. Blackwell. (1998) ISBN 0-87462-165-8

63. *What Sort of Human Nature? Medieval Philosophy and the Systematics of Christology.* Marilyn McCord Adams. (1999) ISBN 0-87462-166-6

ISBN 0-87462-170-4

9 780874 621709

51500

About the Aquinas Lecture Series

The Annual St. Thomas Aquinas Lecture Series began at Marquette University in the spring of 1937. Ideal for classroom use, library additions, or private collections, the Aquinas Lecture Series has received international acceptance by scholars, universities, and libraries. Clothbound in maroon cloth with gold stamped covers. Uniform style and price ($15 each). Some reprints with soft covers. Complete set (67 Titles) (ISBN 0-87462-150-X) receives a 40% discount. New standing orders receive a 30% discount. Regular reprinting keeps all volumes available. Ordering information (purchase orders, checks, and major credit cards accepted):

Marquette University Press
 30 Amberwood Parkway
P.O. Box 2139
Ashland OH 44805
    Order Toll-Free (800) 247-6553
    FAX: (419) 281 6883

Editorial Address:
Dr. Andrew Tallon, Director
Marquette University Press
Box 1881
Milwaukee WI 53201-1881
Tel: (414) 288-7298 FAX: (414) 288-3300
email: andrew.tallon@marquette.edu.

http://www.mu.edu/mupress/